W9-AGH-479

THE BALLET BOOK

THE BALLET BOOK

Learning
and Appreciating
the Secrets of
Dance

AMERICAN BALLET THEATRE

NANCY ELLISON
TEXT BY HANNA RUBIN

UNIVERSE

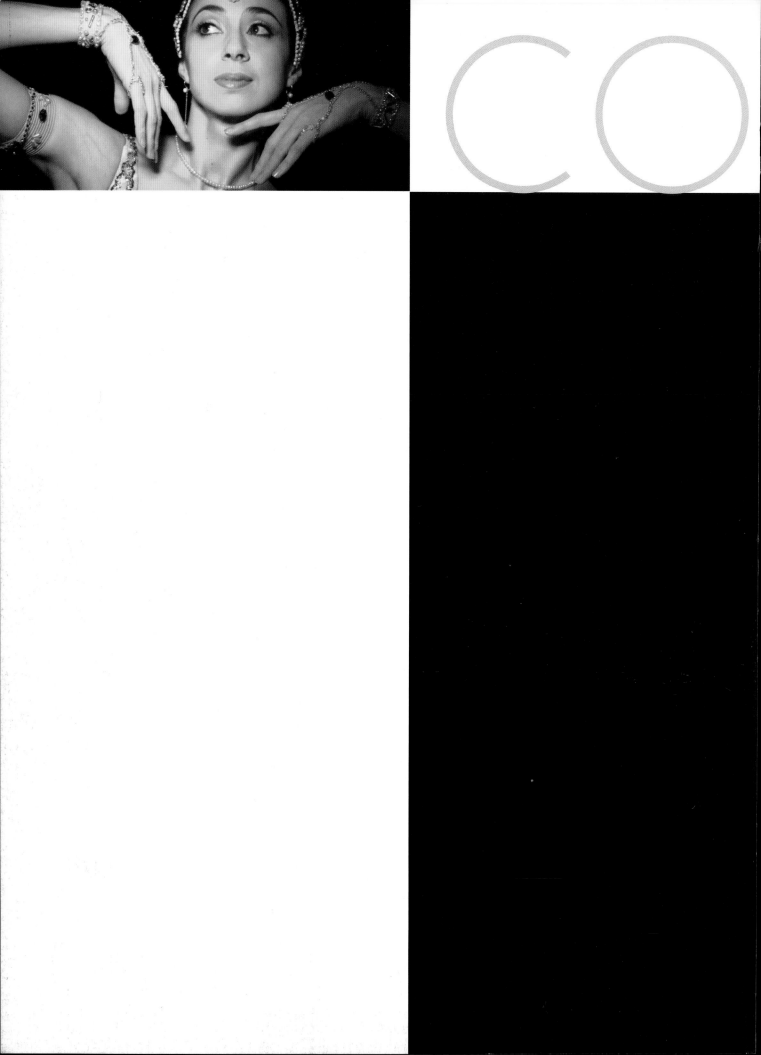

CO

NTENTS

FOREWORD BY
KEVIN MCKENZIE   7

INTRODUCTION   9

BEGIN WITH A DREAM   13
Starting Out

POSITIONS   21
A Selection of the Fundamentals   25

CLASSWORK   39
Before Class   45
Shoes   47
Stretching   51
Training, Health, and Injury Prevention   57
At the Barre   59
Center work   73
Jump   81

REHEARSAL   91
Line   95
Delicacy   101
Elevation   103
Consistency   105
Musicality   107
Expressiveness   109
Amplitude   111
Dynamism   113
Staging a Ballet   117

CHOREOGRAPHY   127
Valentine by Lar Lubovitch   133
Collaboration   137

Setting   143
Gong by Mark Morris   145
Partnering   147
The Touring Life   155

PERFORMANCE   157
Preparing   163
The Virtuoso Dancer   169
The Bravura Dancer   173
The Noble Dancer   177
The Adagio Ballerina   183
The Allegro Ballerina   187
Character and Mime   191
The Ballets   197
Giselle   201
La Bayadère   207
The Sleeping Beauty   215
Swan Lake   219
The Nutcracker   223
Don Quixote   225
Le Corsaire   227
Grand Pas Classique   235
Apollo   237
The Prodigal Son   239
Diana and Actaeon   241
The Dream   243
La Fille Mal Gardée   245
Romeo and Juliet   251
Onegin   255
Manon   257
The Leaves are Fading   259

FAREWELL   261
A Prima Ballerina Retires

First published in the United States of America in 2003
by UNIVERSE PUBLISHING
A Division of Rizzoli International Publications, Inc.
300 Park Avenue South
New York, NY 10010

2003 2004 2005 2006 / 10 9 8 7 6 5 4 3 2 1

Designed by Chuck Davidson
Text by Hanna Rubin
Printed in the United States

ISBN: 0-7893-0869-X (PB)
        0-7893-0865-7 (HC)

Library of Congress Catalog Control Number: 2002115746

'm often asked to explain American Ballet Theatre's philosophy. Our approach is best summed up by the three words of our name. We are American in the sense that we make the most exciting, vibrant, and universal of statements. The medium in which we make it is ballet, and the nature of that expression is theatrical. Our aim is to engage the audience's emotions.

What we say as a company can't be put in a box. We've always had an eclectic group of dancers and a varied repertory, and it's become an identity of its own after 60 years. In many ways, our repertory and style encompass the whole history of ballet from its beginnings through yesterday.

Ballet is an art form that requires incredible discipline for a dancer to achieve his or her goals. It's my hope that this book will help readers understand what happens behind the scenes in the life of a dancer, what that discipline really requires. I also hope that it will draw in those who might be intimidated by ballet's image. Dance is a primal form of communication that everyone understands. Like any other kind of dance, ballet's power is its ability to let you recognize something about yourself. It speaks to people. I defy anyone to come to the ballet and say it doesn't move them. Enjoy this book, and enjoy ABT.

Kevin McKenzie, Artistic Director
American Ballet Theatre

7

Everyone who falls in love with ballet can remember the performance where it happened. It's that moment when dance, art, and music fused into one perfect whole. It's thrilling and inspiring and instantly addictive.

Years of training, effort, and commitment go into mastering ballet's vocabulary as a dancer. And while ballet's traditions and history may seem rarified, ballet is a dynamic art form that continues to evolve. At this moment in a studio somewhere, a dancer and a choreographer are working to take ballet in a fresh, yet unimagined direction.

This book explores some of ballet's fundamentals through the lens of a major ballet company at work. From the demands of class to the rigors of rehearsal to the exhilaration of performance, the dancers of American Ballet Theatre demonstrate all the effort and artistry that go into performing ballet. By the end, a reader will learn and appreciate ballet's secrets, demands, and rewards, and even more.

A KING'S PASSION

The steps we now know as ballet evolved out of seventeenth-century court dances. France's Louis XIV, the Sun King, was an excellent dancer. With his patronage, dancing masters became favored courtiers. They staged long spectacles, choreographing interludes that used steps based on the now-familiar five positions of the feet. Around 1700, some of the steps were codified and recorded in manuals. In the same period, a royal academy of dance, which one day would become the Paris Opera Ballet, was established. It became the first ballet school and French remains the language of ballet to this day.

Ballet in its infancy did not resemble what we now admire and enjoy watching. No one danced on pointe and men, not women, wore tutu-style costumes. Gradually, as the decades went by, the emphasis shifted from male to female dancers. Ballerinas began to go on pointe early in the nineteenth century, and as their feats drew appreciative audiences, they executed ever-more complicated steps. One famous ballerina of the day, the Italian star Marie Taglioni, celebrated for the lightness and grace of her dancing, has been credited with making pointework more than mere acrobatics. Soon she had many rivals.

By mid-century, ballet was a popular form of entertainment, and ballerinas had international followings. The Russian imperial court, long an admirer of all things French, imported French dancers and choreographers, called ballet masters, to stage ballets in St. Petersburg. Among them was Marius Petipa, who would create a new paradigm for ballet in works such as *La Bayadère* and *Swan Lake*. Ballet flourished in the twilight of Tsarist Russia, but its heyday ended even before the Russian Revolution. The decades that followed World War I found dance artists from the Russian, French, and Italian traditions fanning out across Europe, influenced by the forces of modernism and change. It was a time of great creativity and innovation, and when war again seemed imminent, many of ballet's greatest talents came to the United States.

NEW WORLD BALLET

Two major companies that would shape American ballet had their earliest incarnations in New York City in those years between the two World Wars: eventually one would be known as New York City Ballet and the other as American Ballet Theatre. At NYCB, George Balanchine, a visionary Russian choreographer, teamed up with patron Lincoln Kirstein to create a company and a school that showcased his works. ABT, in turn, was the brainchild of Lucia Chase, a wealthy American with a passion for ballet. She entered a partnership with impresario Richard Pleasant to present an eclectic repertory of new American works and classics.

ABT's productions continue to mix old and new. The company often commissions new pieces, but also presents a number of full-length story ballets. While no ballet company in the world is truly like any other, ABT has theatrical roots similar to such European companies as England's Royal Ballet and Russia's Kirov Ballet. It's an old-fashioned approach, one that preserves a star system and production values. It also means that audiences have the opportunity to see virtuoso dancers and to experience the gamut of ballet as a dance idiom.

At NYCB, the emphasis remains on the training and choreography that Balanchine created during his long tenure. The School of American Ballet teaches Balanchine technique, and the dancers often go into the company or into companies that were started by Balanchine dancers, such as the San Francisco Ballet. The Balanchine style cannot be distilled into a few adjectives, but it requires speed, athleticism, and musicality.

DIFFERENT STYLES,
DIFFERENT SCHOOLS

A school usually defines a company's style. At the moment, ABT does not have a school of its own, but recruits dancers from schools and companies all over the world. While more companies are taking this approach, there are still distinct differences in national style that stem from training.

The English style, fostered at the Royal Ballet School, often seems demure compared to others. Training includes pantomime and history of ballet, and a lot of attention to footwork and the presentation of the foot, notes ABT ballet mistress Georgina Parkinson, a former ballerina with the Royal Ballet. During her years at the school, the emphasis was on a very secure base for movement, and an overall restraint in presentation, which can still be noted today.

The Russian style is known for its lovely port de bras, or arms, and the ballerina's regal carriage. "Your arms must be pretty and soft," recalls former principal dancer and ABT coach Irina Kolpakova. "We were taught to feel the pose as well as hold it." Kolpakova studied at The Vaganova Academy, the renowned Kirov Ballet and other Russian companies. She points to the emphasis placed there on musicality. "Your movement and the music should be phrased the same way. Everything from your toes to your fingertips must be very light, and when the music changes, your jump should too."

French ballet tradition, which has been shaped at The Paris Opera Ballet's famous academy, dictates impeccable line and elegance. It's a very different look from the British or Russian style. There is a certain chic to the ballerina's presentation. Dramatic interpretation receives less emphasis in the French schooling, but technical brilliance is recognized and promoted from the start.

IN THE COMPANY

Most ballet companies have the same structure: a corps de ballet at the bottom of the hierarchy, soloists in the middle, and principals in the leading roles. While traditionally a dancer begins in the corps de ballet, an exceptionally talented one may enter as a soloist. Just as often, a dancer will begin in the corps de ballet and remain there throughout his or her professional career. Rising from the ranks takes a combination of effort, talent, and luck.

Stardom comes to only a few, and a dancer's career usually ends by the time he or she turns 40. Still, few dancers would trade ballet for something else. Performing ballet is one career choice motivated by pure, intense love. And audiences know it. "No matter how much you talk about ballet, there is nothing that equals the excitement of seeing it," says former ABT ballerina Susan Jaffe. "There's no way to describe the experience of watching a great artist. Dancers struggle through hard work and experience to pour themselves into ballet. We in the audience do not know why we are moved when we watch them. It's all in that moment. It may be a fleeting emotion, but every time, it's a gift."

That gift can only happen in the theater. Ballet is a living art, and no video can ever replicate the excitement of seeing it, the rush of emotion that you feel, the sheer thrill of being in the audience and giving yourself entirely to the moment, to the dancer, and to the dance.

BEGIN
DRE

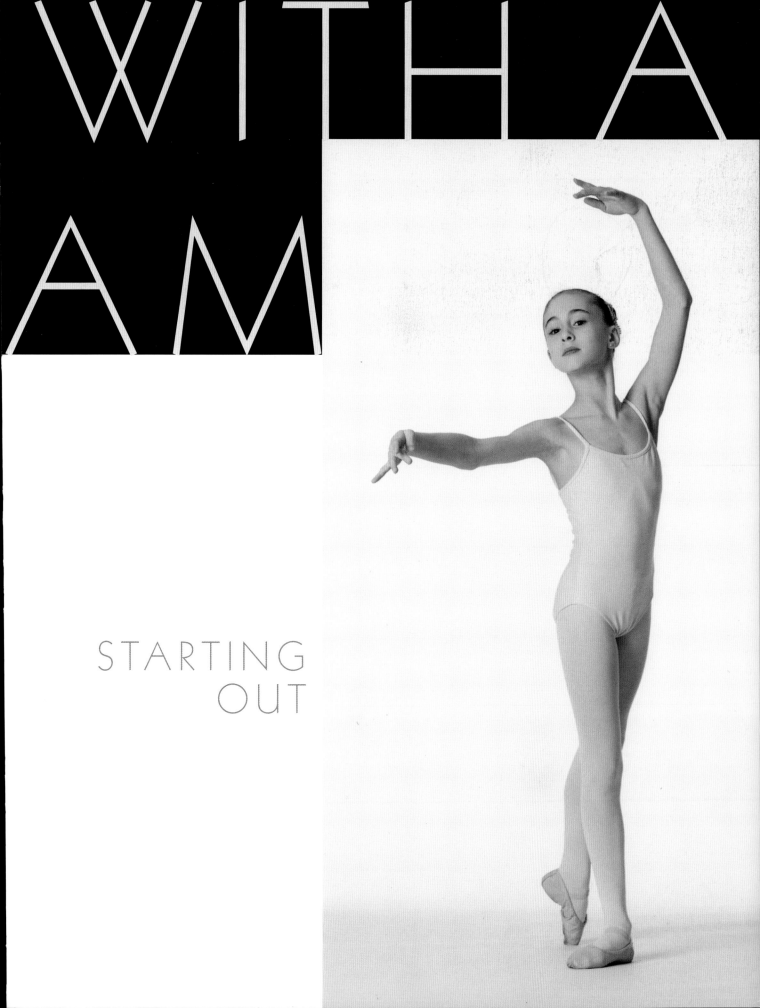

WITH A WHAM

STARTING OUT

Professionals begin when they are quite young—seven or eight is typical. They don't know it will become their passion. One dancer began studying ballet after watching his sister's class and thinking the time would go faster if he did the steps too. Another dancer took class because she wanted to become a professional ice skater and ballet helped to refine her performances. When an injury prevented her from continuing to skate, she refocused her energy on ballet. Today, both are principals with ABT.

Teachers, professionals, and students agree that you should pursue ballet from love, not ambition. "The best students aren't forcing themselves, they're indulging themselves," says Lupe Serrano, a former principal dancer who teaches an ABT company class. Whether a student gives up ballet in a few years or makes it a career, mastering the steps should bring its own gratification. Studying ballet must fulfill a cherished dream. The allure of leotards, tutus, and slippers will wear thin quickly.

STARTING OUT

The first steps that a dancer learns are the basic positions that provide the foundation for everything that will come. These include the five positions of the feet, the different ways to extend the leg while maintaining the correct position of the foot—from tendu to battement to arabesque—and the various positions of the arms. Dancers learn the different turns and jumps, and begin to combine all of these steps into simple patterns. They will spend a few years becoming adept at these steps. Even when dancers reach professional level, they will always return to these same steps in class.

For anyone who took ballet classes as a child, professional classes will seem familiar. The class that the top-ranked dancers take every morning covers virtually the same ground as the one a ten-year-old takes at a ballet school. Like youngsters, professionals begin at the barre, warming their bodies up with pliés (see "Positions" in the following pages), and slowly building to more complicated feats of coordination and balance. After perhaps 45 minutes, the dancers move to the center, like their young counterparts, to try a similar series of movements without the barre as an aid. The pace of this center work begins slowly, but picks up speed as the combinations become more elaborate and include bigger jumps. By the end, the dancers eat up the floor diagonally with their leaps and pirouettes the same way that the youngest students do. While a class for eight- or ten-year-olds may be shorter and simpler than one for professionals—in some schools they may last an hour instead of the standard 90 minutes—the steps and the progress from barre work to jumping will be jumping will be virtually identical.

All ballet classes are performed to music, whether live or taped. Teaching young students to listen for the beat and pick up the tempo, to time their steps to the music's phrasing, is an essential part of training. Teachers will often request that students perform combinations at the barre and in the center that require them to count out the number of repetitions and time them to the music's beat. It's a way to help students start to synchronize their movements to the music.

GOING ON POINTE

In the first years, female students build their strength, firm up their posture, and prepare their bodies for the challenge of going on pointe. "You don't rush into complicated movements," notes Serrano. "You should learn the whole vocabulary, including folk and modern. Nothing makes up for careful groundwork." Over time, essentials like turning out from the hips, pointing the foot, extending the leg or arm fully and holding the head correctly must become instinctive. Only then is the dancer ready to move ahead.

It also takes several years of building strength in the ankles, feet, and legs before a young dancer is ready to go on point and a teacher is the best judge of when a student truly has attained the necessary strength. Many of the exercises that a dancer performs in class, especially the exercises that require a dancer to repeatedly point and flex their feet, to maintain their balance and to find their center of gravity, must become second nature to their muscles before they first can roll up on pointe, holding on to the barre as they rise slowly to the tips of their toes. For some dancers, achieving this level of strength may take longer. Most students begin practicing pointework in 45-minute or hour-long classes, slowly becoming accustomed to the demands on their sense of balance and their feet and calves, while by contrast professionals may spend six or eight hours on pointe in the course of a day of rehearsals and performance.

It takes a while before most students stop sinking into their toe shoes and master the embarrassing wobbling. It's also a time when many dancers find their bodies changing. Between ages of eleven and thirteen, puberty begins. The body that a dancer develops may not permit her to achieve the line that ballet demands. "Your success all depends on your final physicality," says Serrano. "That's why children should be children, and not give up their education and a regular life." While professional ballet isn't limited to a single body type, most companies take a hard look at dancers' proportions when they audition and gauge carefully how they will read from the stage. Puberty is also a time when dancers who may be possessed of a natural sense of rhythm suddenly feel out of synch with their bodies.

Though students can learn to dance to the music, few can learn musicality, that elusive trait which allows dancers to become one with the music's phrasing, to end each step naturally on the beat, and to remember the structure of a piece effortlessly and pace themselves accordingly. It's one of those traits, like a long neck or great flexibility, that are a given.

Sometimes adults who have studied ballet as children, or simply admire the art, want to take class. Many colleges and universities with performing arts programs offer adult ballet classes that the public can attend as well. Adult ballet builds poise and confidence. It gives students a sense of control and mastery, and it improves posture. And a 90-minute class definitely counts as a workout. Adult students may find it harder to build to the level of strength that permits them to try pointework. There are also health considerations: anyone with a history of knee injuries or back problems should not consider it. But whether an adult pursues the discipline of ballet all the way to pointe, adult study is a wonderful way to enjoy ballet by living it as well as watching it.

SUMMER INTENSIVE PROGRAMS

If a young dancer has shown promise and dedication that's noticeable to his or her teachers, buckling down for the unvarying routine of class as many as six days a week, he or she may want to take a summer intensive course at a ballet academy. Most summer programs have residential facilities, and most require auditions. Summer intensives allow dancers to build their skills in areas a local school may not cover, such as partnering or character dancing. Schools that offer professional-level training also require auditions, so the sooner a young dancer with serious ambitions becomes accustomed to them, the better.

The audition process filters every stage of a dancer's studies. A student quickly learns whether the training he or she has received will stand up to professional scrutiny. If the preparation proves sound, and a student gets admitted, he or she will find that summer intensive programs tend to be rigorous and competitive. Going to one may help a young dancer decide if he or she really wants to make the commitment that advanced study demands.

The tradition of summer intensive study began in New York at New York City's School of American Ballet many decades ago, when the school could not offer a full-time residential option to promising students around the country. A summer program offered at least a beginning to young dancers who lived far from New

York. Today, the school has a prestigious residential program, and its summer intensive course has become an informal extended audition for places in it. American Ballet Theatre has yet to develop a similar school, but it too has a summer intensive program. This allows the company to spot promising students from around the country and support their continued studies in their hometowns with scholarships. Some eventually may end up in the Studio Company, ABT's training ground for preprofessional dancers, which functions as a junior company. At sixteen, a dancer can join the Studio Company, where they will have the opportunity to perform constantly, even touring abroad. The Studio Company is also a place where up-and-coming choreographers can try out their new works, staging their ballet with the dancers for the first time.

SCHOOLS AND ADVANCED TRAINING

There is no formal system in the United States for accrediting dance academies. Standards vary widely. For this reason, the School of American Ballet, long a source of talent for the New York City Ballet, does not maintain a list of preferred schools among its admissions criteria. Parents and students must rely on their own judgment.

One question to ask in selecting a school is how many students go on to advanced training, and where? If a school has a long record of sending dancers on to other programs, or has produced several dancers that have gone on to join established companies, it's a good indicator that they offer a reliable grounding. Many of the country's most prominent professional companies also maintain ballet academies. Students who live near enough may opt to take classes there, and ultimately apply for a slot in their full-time residential programs.

"The best students aren't forcing themselves, they're indulging themselves."

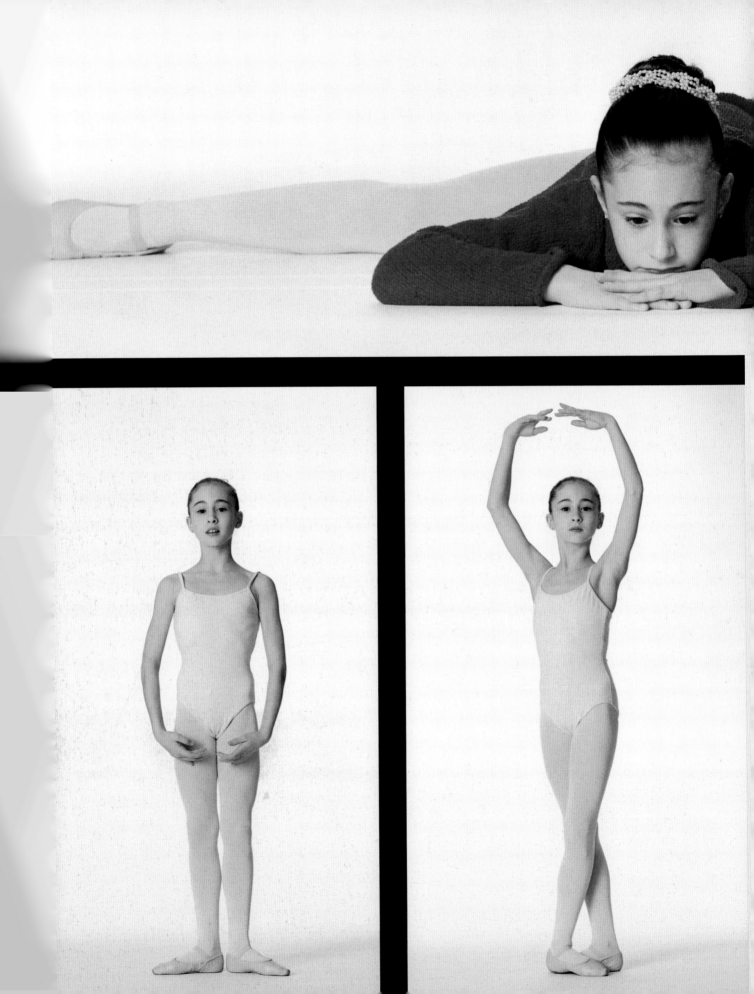

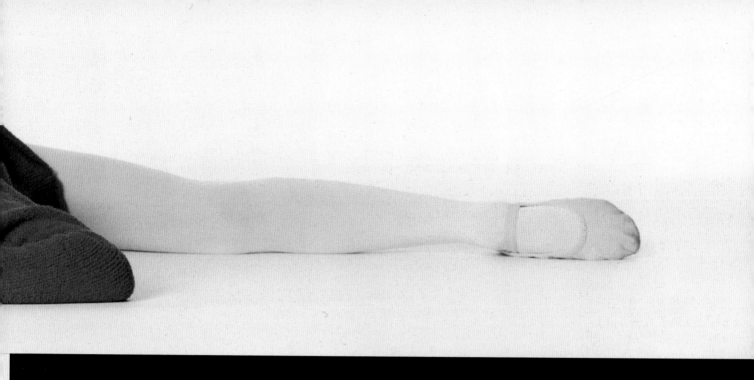

Students may begin studying ballet as young as six or seven, although most start when they are eight or a little older. If a child wishes to become a professional dancer, by eleven years old they should consider taking classes five days a week.

A student at New York City's Ballet Academy East, Alexandra Dobles, 12, started when she was 7 and now goes to classes six days a week, as well as attending the Pennsylvania Youth Ballet's summer intensive program. Her professional appearances have included ABT's production of *Le Corsaire*. "If you really love to dance, it's fun," she says of her dance-focused schedule. "It can't feel like work, or you'll never be able to express yourself when you do it." In these photos, Alexandra demonstrates the correct stance in first, fifth, and fourth positions: head up, back straight, and softly curving arms extending through the fingertips. Above, Alexandra shows the flexibility that ballet

POSIT

In the following pages are photographs of some basic ballet positions that are the key elements in many combinations and strengthen and develop the body to go on to perform the complex sequences of steps that ballet demands.

Ballet begins with the five basic positions of the feet. First codified in the seventeenth century, every ballet step begins and ends in one or another. There are also standard positions for the arms, or port de bras, and the head. This is because classical form involves the entire body, says Clinton Luckett, an artistic associate and teacher at American Ballet Theatre. "There is no dichotomy between the arms and the legs. They are far more expressive together. The function of the positions is to provide channels for energy and movement."

Class always begins with pliés. "What dance form doesn't bend at the knee? You can't dance without pliés," Luckett explains. Pliés stretch the Achilles tendon and limber up dancers' legs. They are the take-off for every jump. "Pliés are the down before the up," says Luckett. With pliés, the knees should stay outward, not forward. The body should be moving out, not down, and the back should always stay straight through the continuous movement. The "up" in ballet is called relevé. It describes when a dancer goes on demi-pointe, which looks like standing on tip-toe, or halfway up to full pointe. This movement involves the whole body. "You rise as though there were helium in your head," says Luckett.

Next comes extending the leg out from the body, while one arm is on the barre and the other is extended toward the room's center to establish a balance. These include tendus, where the toe of the extended foot stays on the floor as it points front, back and side; this is similar to a rond de jambe à terre, which draws a circle on the floor with the toe of the pointed extended foot. Then come the battements dégagés, where the toe leaves or disengages from the floor in a series of brushing kicks, and frappés, where the ankle of the extended foot is flexed as the leg is extended forward, back, and side. Gradually, the leg builds higher and higher in développés, to the front, back, and side.

The positions of the body integrate several elements into one stance. À la quatrième devant, for instance, has a dancer facing front in fourth position with his or her right foot pointed ahead and the arms in second position. It is the starting point for many combinations, or sequences of steps, and it's a position that looks collected and ready. Holding the body upright, but not stiffly, is essential for executing steps. "Slouching isn't a strong, clear channel for energy," says Luckett. "It's not defined enough to make an impression. It looks mediocre."

That alignment and carriage are critical elements for poses like arabesques, where the dancer stands on one leg and holds the other lifted and pointed behind them, and attitudes, where the lifted extended leg is bent at an angle. "An arabesque is like the swoop on a Nike logo," says Luckett. "The energy goes forward and backward. You're stretching away from your center in opposing directions." Luckett describes an attitude as that same energy circling in a spiral.

The basic positions have a near-infinite number of variations. Taken all together, they make up the language of ballet. Break down any step and you will find the elementary positions and movements you learn at the barre.

There are some positions that cannot be performed without a partner, and if you reach an advanced level you will learn them. They, too, however, are based on the same fundamentals that begin every ballet class. Partnering is about timing, about finding the center of balance and not throwing the other person off his or hers. "Partnering is mostly about helping the woman maintain her position longer than she could by herself," says Luckett. "It's a beautiful demonstration of the male-female dynamic. When you lift a ballerina, you take her physically into space to a place where she can't go alone, and where she wants to go."

In the end, ballet involves mastering a variety of positions, but those positions are not ballet. "Classical ballet is the singularly most rigorously developed form of dance," says Luckett. "Most people confuse the form for ballet itself." It's much more, as ballet dancers will tell you, and as these pages will show.

From left to right, the basic five positions: first position, where the heels are together and the toes point out; second position, where the feet are spread apart and the knees are aligned with the toes; third position, where the feet are partly crossed and the heel of the front foot rests near the arch of the back foot; fourth position, where the feet are crossed and there is space between the two feet; and fifth position, where the legs are crossed and the feet are aligned, touching toe to heel.

A

B

C

F

G

H

J

K

L

D

E

I

A selection of some
fundamental positions
and movements of the
barre exercises are
shown here. Listed
below, from left to right

A. Demi-plié in first
   position
B. Grand plié in first
   position
C. Grand plié in
   second position

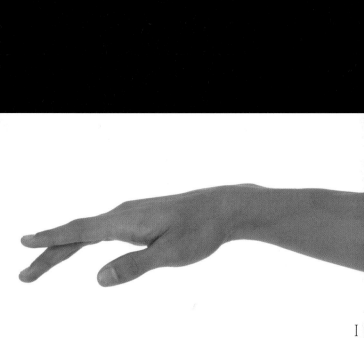

I

The arabesques at left show both the incorrect and correct ways to execute the position. In the photo at far left (E), the supporting leg is pointing forward. The leg should be turned out, as it is in (F).

The two photos at far left, (G) and (H), show common mistakes in how dancers hold their hands. In both, the fingers are held stiffly and awkwardly. Instead, the energy of the movement should flow away from the body through the fingertips, as it does in the photo at near left (I).

A

B

C

D

E

F

H

I

G

ARABESQUE AND ATTITUDE

The working leg
extends in a straight
line in arabesque.
Attitude is when the
leg is bent. Listed
below and illustrated at
left are several different
types of arabesque and
attitude positions.

A. First Arabesque
B. Arabesque penchée
C. Second Arabesque
D. Third Arabesque
E. Fourth Arabesque
F. First Arabesque
G. Arabesque en plié
H. Attitude croisé
I. Attitude effacé

B

C

PARTNERING

These supported positions, a Fish dive, a supported arabesque, and a lunge are studied at an advanced level of training.

The Fish dive (A) is a term used in supported work in which the woman is supported by the man in a poisson position, a position of the body in which the legs are crossed in the fifth position and held tightly together with the back arched. He may hold her above his head in a horizontal fish dive or she may fall from a sitting position on his shoulder.

The First Arabesque (B) has the man supporting the woman as she executes an arabesque. The position of her body, in profile, is supported on one leg, which can be straight or demi-plié.

A lunge (C) is often the coda to a series of assisted pirouettes.

A

C

B

D

E

G

THE POSITIONS OF THE BODY

In a Effacé devant (A) the dancer stands at an oblique angle to the audience, facing one of the two corners of the room. The term means "crossed in front."

In Croisé derrière (B) the torso is straight and the high arm is on the same side as the extended leg.

À la quatrième devant (C) is "to the fourth position front." The feet should be placed in the fourth position, the arms in the second position.

À la quatrième derrière (D) is "to the fourth position back."

The term écarté means "separated, thrown apart," and in the Écarté devant (E) the leg that is closer to the audience is pointed in the second position à terre or raised to the second position in the air.

Effacé devant (F) means "shaded in front." The arms are placed in attitude (bent), the arm that is low is on the same side as the leg that is extended.

Croisé derrière (G) is the opposite of Effacé devant—the arms are placed in attitude, but it is the arm that is high that is on the same side as the leg that is extended.

F

PETIT AND ALLEGRO JUMPS

The most dramatic jumps are performed by male dancers. They have the muscular development to propel themselves in the air and hang there for several seconds, sometimes executing a series of turns, or performing airborne leg beats. The free-form versions of classical jumps pictured here, such as the soubresaut (top far left) and the sissonne (bottom right), run from little (petit) to big (grand). Each jump has its own preparation, beginning in a plié and ending in one to cushion the impact. The landing plié becomes the impetus for the next jump.

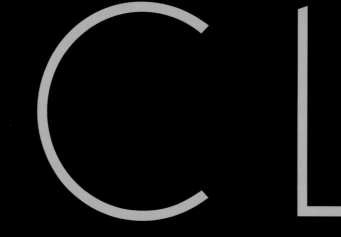

THE
FOUNDATION

ASS-
ORK

Class is the foundation for performing ballet for both young students and seasoned professionals. It's a touchstone for even the most experienced dancers, a daily review of the building blocks of movement that give ballet its formal structure. Every member of a professional company takes class each morning, from the most celebrated dancers to the newest member of the corps. "If you skip class one day, you know it. If you skip class two days, your teacher knows it. And if you skip class three days, the audience knows it," goes the saying attributed to Rudolf Nureyev. Lupe Serrano likens class to practicing scales on the piano.

While attending company class is not required, and some dancers prefer to take class outside the company, most members like the opportunity to work with the rest of their fellow dancers. Where private classes for youngsters generally should not exceed 20 students so the teacher can give thorough corrections, company class may be far larger, including as many as 40 students. Company class is also where auditions to enter the company take place. Ballet masters will come by to watch aspiring members work alongside the others. "It's the best way to tell, by having dancers right there among the company. You'll see pretty quickly if they can meet the standard," says Serrano.

Held each morning, a company class follows the established pattern of ballet classes all over the world. There's usually 45 minutes of warming up at the barre, a half-hour of center work to build balance and control, and a final half-hour of jumps to build energy and warm up the entire body. While class has clear physical benefits, its larger purpose is to entrench the fundamentals of ballet in the dancers' bodies and minds. "It's all about keeping your technique clean," says Serrano, using a favorite ballet adjective to describe the combination of precision, poise, and ability. "You have to practice over and over to be able to do that."

THE DANCE STUDIO

Class usually takes place in a studio lined with mirrors on one, and sometimes three sides and a wooden floor. The mirrors are for dancers to check their positions and correct themselves, and the floor must be wood so that it gives a little when the dancers jump, just like the floor of a high school gym. Dancing on cement, even if it's overlaid with flooring, is a recipe for injury. Some studios have the barre attached to the walls, while others use freestanding barres that can be moved to the side when the first part of class is over. In a professional-level class, there is usually a piano accompanist whom the teacher directs to use different music according to how she or he is pacing the class. At the student level, some teachers work with taped music. Teachers vary their lesson emphasis according to the students' level of experience, and in the case of company class, according to what choreography is being rehearsed. Some teachers give less time at the barre or perhaps trim back the jumping at the end, but each section of class moves from slow, or adagio, to fast, or allegro.

CLASS ETIQUETTE
Strict politeness is in order during class. Dancers should show respect for those who are older or more senior, and behave courteously toward their peers. That means that principals, or for that matter, senior students, choose where they want to stand in class; it's not appropriate to preempt them. The teacher deserves the dancers' complete attention; he or she should not have to repeat instructions. Practicing on the sides when dancers are waiting for their turn to cross the floor is disturbing. It shows more consideration of others to simply stand quietly. If a dancer bumps into someone during a combination, they should apologize whether or not they are at fault.

TURNOUT
When dancers take their place at the barre, they usually begin in first position with their legs turned out. Some dancers can achieve a 180-degree turnout with their legs. "It's an extreme position," notes ABT artistic director Kevin McKenzie, pointing out that the practice began in the court of the Sun King, Louis XIV, an enthusiastic dancer who was proud of his legs and believed that turned-out positions showed them off to advantage. This essential element of ballet demands changing the body's natural alignment, which has both feet pointing forward rather than to the side. It takes time to achieve the degree of turnout that basic positions require. Some dancers will force their turnout, and that can create a sway backed look, and ultimately, lumbar back problems.

Remember that turnout begins at the hips, not the ankles. Stretching before class (see "Stretch") will enable a dancer to turn out more fully and more easily. To achieve maximum turnout, muscles must be stretched, molded, and stretched again. When a dancer has a good turnout, it creates a balanced look and it means that the dancer's whole body has been properly aligned. Everything is tucked in, back and front, and the dancer has found his or her center of gravity.

THE BARRE
Class always begins at the barre. It's a warmup for what's to come, a careful review of deep knee bends, and tendus, which are leg extensions in a variety of positions. The barre allows dancers to check their alignment, to review their port de bras or arm positions, to begin the process of balancing and controlling movement that will

continue once they move to the center.

Ask three teachers of ballet class the barre's function, and you will hear three different answers. It may seem a matter of nuance, but the use of the barre remains controversial. "The barre is never a support, merely a guideline," says McKenzie. Victor Barbee, the company's Assistant Artistic Director who teaches class from time to time, sees it differently. "The barre is there to support the dancer while he or she perfects the positions and strengthen technique," he says. Artistic associate Clinton Luckett, who teaches class to ABT's Studio Company, believes there's no definitive answer. "Some teachers encourage you to take your hand off," he says. "They feel you should be able to do all the positions without the barre. Others feel you need the support of the barre to establish your natural alignment and strengthen it. Certainly, you shouldn't prop yourself up with the barre; use it as a reference point to find the invisible plumb line of your center of gravity."

CENTERWORK

After working at the barre, the class moves to the center of the studio. The dancers begin slowly, perhaps building their balance by moving their "working" leg through front, back, and side développés. As its name implies, these positions are achieved slowly through a gradual unfurling of the limb so that the fullest extension is reached. This section of class, which Serrano calls "the barre without the barre," focuses on building control. Dancers face the mirror, checking their posture, arm and hand positions, and the angle of their legs, making small adjustments. They will extend an arabesque to a slightly higher angle, adjust their arms to frame their head more gracefully, while the teacher gradually begins to pick up the pace of the combinations. When this part of the class is over, the female members of the corps de ballet often will run to the sides of the studio and put on their toe shoes, since they will have less time on their pointes during the hours of rehearsal that follow than soloist or principal dancers.

POINTEWORK, PIROUETTES, AND SPOTTING

In a company class, principals and soloists will often spend the entire 90 minutes in ballet slippers, especially if they have a heavy schedule of rehearsals or performances ahead. Working in slippers, which is also called demi-pointe, strengthens smaller muscles in the feet and the back of the calf, which bears the brunt of a dancer's weight when she or he is standing or turning on one leg. Pirouetting, or turning on one leg, on demi-pointe allows dancers to improve their spotting ability before going up on pointe, where the turns are faster and less easily controlled. To avoid becoming dizzy, dancers must keep their heads to the front while their bodies execute the turn, then whip their heads around at the end to complete it. Dancers are often told to pick a particular spot in the room and keep their eyes on it to the very last second before bringing their head around.

REPETITIONS

As class progresses, the teacher will ask the dancers to perform more complex combinations of steps. Each sequence will involve repeating movement patterns that are increasingly airborne. Even at the barre, however, dancers will be asked to repeat sets of steps in groups of four or eight in time to the music. "You must repeat the movements to warm up properly," Serrano explains. "When you move to the center, it takes repetition to make it better. Nobody does it perfectly the first time." Watching company class, you often see the most famous principals eagerly waiting their turn behind members of the corps to whip through a combination again and again. "Repetition gives the dancers the freedom to expand their abilities," Serrano explains. "You can push yourself, you can make mistakes, you can do it once more, and a teacher is there to give corrections."

JUMPS

The last half-hour of class becomes a burst of energy as dancers leap across the studio on the diagonal, making maximum use of the space. Jumps come in two sizes, small and big, petit allegro and grand allegro. Both men and women perform petit allegro steps such as soubresauts, or little jumps, in fifth position. But it is in grand allegro that men really shine. Only men perform the expansive turns in the air which leave audiences gasping. For them, too, are reserved the scissor kicks (sissonnes), and leg-touching leaps (cabrioles). Women may equal a man's elevation when they perform a grand jeté, or leap onto one foot, but they don't have the same physical power to propel themselves into the air and turn.

At the end of every class, another tradition continues—the dancers applaud the teacher, a mark of their respect. In more old-fashioned schools, they may curtsy or bow. This is making a "révérance," which reflects the dancers' recognition of ballet's long oral tradition. The teacher represents that history, which is passed down from one dancer to another, from body to body, every day in class. Nothing deserves more reverence in the world of ballet.

The dancers start to filter in about 20 minutes before class begins. Some come as much as a half-hour early to begin the laborious process of stretching and warming up. They chat quietly as they put on their shoes and begin to flex. Some wear the black leotards and light tights that most nonprofessional students wear, but others favor baggy warmups in breathable materials. Dancers often layer their warmup outfits, gradually peeling T-shirts, scarves, and sweats as class progresses.

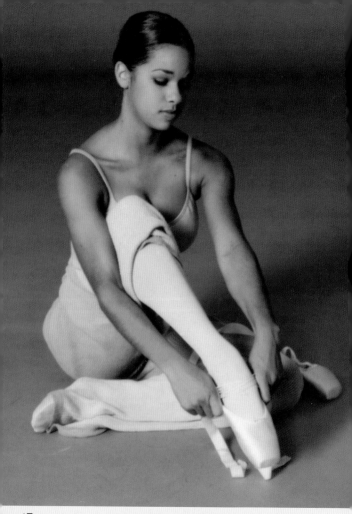

Once ballet dancers join major companies, their shoes are made to order by a manufacturer of their preference who has their specific measurements. Pointe shoes are made of surprisingly flimsy materials: cardboard, for the toe box, a particle board shank or tongue for the sole, and satin covering. A few dancers recently have turned to a new generation of padded high-tech pointe shoes that are based on athletic shoe design. These create a more cushioned box for the toe. Most, though, like Misty Copeland, left, still use traditional shoes, which may offer less support, but have an elegant silhouette that adheres closely to the shape of the foot.

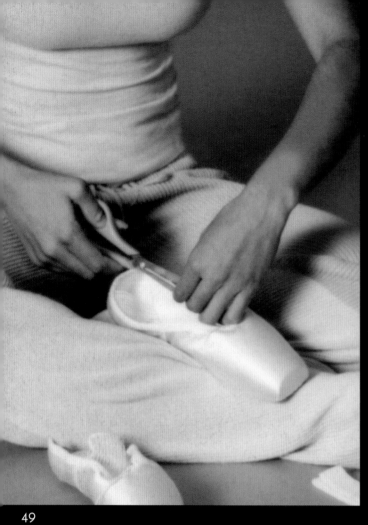

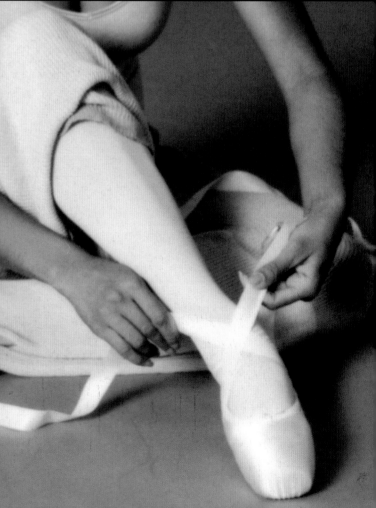

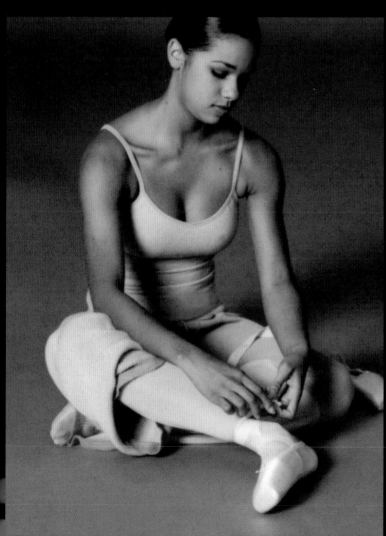

For dancers, their feet are virtually a fetish. Each dancer has a ritual when it comes to breaking in a new pair of shoes. But the process is critical for ballerinas who spend so much time on pointe. Misty, a young corps de ballet dancer, follows a set routine with each new pair she gets—and she wears out several a week. She cuts off the ribbons and elastics at the ankles, and resews them in a better position to give her feet the most comfort and support. Copeland doesn't pad the toes of her pointe shoes, because she feels it makes them bulky and unattractive. Instead, she cuts off the satin at the tip to make the toe surface rougher and give it greater traction when she's on pointe. She will step on her shoes to soften them up—some dancers go so far as hammering them— and she cuts the shank or tongue of the particle board in half to make it more pliable. Only then are the shoes ready to wear.

51

Stretching before class and afterwards holds the key to injury prevention, as does stretching before and after rehearsal. "A stretched muscle is a healthy muscle," says company physiotherapist Peter Marshall. The stretches at left work the hamstrings, which run up the legs from the back of the knee to the hip joint, and enable dancers to achieve more dramatic 180-degree leg extensions. Stretching is also a focusing process for dancers. "You need to be able to isolate individual muscles, but it's also a way to handle nervousness, almost like whittling," says Kevin McKenzie.

Dancers such as these corps de ballet members use various props to help the stretching process, but the barre remains a favorite. Placing one leg on the barre and slowly moving the working leg's extension away from the body is also a hamstring warmup, top left. Some dancers bring giant rubber bands to strengthen their insteps through resistance training, top right. Others bring Styrofoam tubes to "roll out" leg muscles. Working the hip joint improves turnout, bottom right, and stretching calf muscles, bottom left, prevents Achilles tendon injuries.

TRAINING, HEALTH, AND INJURY PREVENTION

Ballet dancers have exceptional muscle tone, fast metabolisms, and tremendous strength. Few will ever suffer from hypertension. However, ballet's strict movement lexicon places unusual stresses on dancers' bodies. Turnout is not a natural position for the legs, nor is pointework. Hyperextended leg positions take their toll on hip joints, as do jumps and turns. Warming up lessens the risk of straining muscles and can ward off common ballet injuries like tibial stress fractures, Achilles tendon tears, or knee dislocations.

The best way to prevent injuries is to dance within your body's limitations, says Peter Marshall, ABT's staff physiotherapist. Marshall points out that few dancers can achieve a 180-degree turnout solely from their hips. Many force a few additional degrees from the ankles down, increasing the possibility that they will lose their balance and roll forward, leading to a tear or strain. "When you're 18 or 19, you feel indestructible. Sometimes it takes several injuries before you listen," Marshall says. "The danger is that you end up with hip or knee arthritis. Older dancers are savvier. They'll mark the steps or the lifts if they have a tight back."

Marshall encourages dancers to allow plenty of time, at least a half-hour, to warm up before class or rehearsal. He suggests including lunges to build up the quadriceps in the thighs, using the barre to stretch hamstrings from knees to buttocks, and doing abdominal-strengthening exercises to improve posture and alignment. To increase a dancer's overall body strength, Marshall may recommend other kinds of training in addition to the regular workout of class.

SWIMMING

Cross-training has become a standard for fitness in recent decades. Marshall points out that swimming provides a full-body workout that causes far less stress on weight-bearing joints than a treadmill or stair machine. It also offers a special benefit for injured dancers. The buoyancy of the water lets them perform movements they can't yet achieve on land, giving a huge psychological boost to the healing process.

PILATES

This exercise regimen offers particular benefits to ballet dancers, since it strengthens the body's ability to support an extreme range of motion by ever-increasing stretches through the use of spring weights.

WEIGHT-TRAINING

Many male dancers opt to work with weights to strengthen back muscles for partnering.

NUTRITION

A dancer's strength and ability doesn't depend solely on his or her physical workout. Marshall believes in fostering a healthy eating regimen. He urges dancers to avoid the caffeinated colas and coffee many use to boost their energy and as an over-the-counter diuretic. "I push water, juices, Gatorade, anything that will replace all the fluid they lose in the course of the day," he says.

Some dancers struggle with their weight and Marshall takes an active role in helping them develop sensible eating habits. "Dancers have got to have protein," he says. "You break down your muscle mass if you don't eat enough." Calcium intake is equally important. An underweight dancer is especially vulnerable because she may stop menstruating, which will affect her estrogen production. Without estrogen, calcium becomes harder for the body to absorb, lowering bone density and increasing the risk of injury. Marshall recommends yogurt, cheese, and milk to build up bone density, which ideally should be higher, not lower than normal in dancers.

FOOT CARE

Dancers' feet are literally a sore point for many. They are prone to injury and even something as ordinary as a callus can have a debilitating effect on a performance. Marshall urges dancers to work over their feet with pumice stones after baths to keep calluses from forming. He frequently gives out toe-spacers to help dancers realign their big toes, which take the bulk of their weight in positions like relevé and can build up bunions and bone spurs. He always keeps Second Skin, a brand of moist gel pads, on hand for blisters, and he urges female dancers to recheck their pointe shoe size as time goes by. Few want to admit that their feet have spread, and will continue squeezing their feet into too-tight shoes, risking injury.

"When you're eighteen or nineteen, you feel indestructible. Sometimes it takes

Ballet class begins with about 45 minutes at the barre. It's a careful progress through a range of motion that gradually involves the entire body. It begins with demi- and grand pliés to turn hips out and warm up leg muscles (see following pages). Next come tendus, ronde de jambe, battements, and développés. As barrework progresses, positions and combinations increase in complexity. At left, members of the corps de ballet in a cambrey, or deep bend forward, in tendu fourth front.

In ballet, all movement emanates from the body's center. "In a great dancer, what's thrilling is that core of strength. It's the still point at the heart of the movement," says Clinton Luckett. To build that core, dancers begin class at the barre, using it to help establish their physical frame of reference and make their bodies a straight vertical column from head to foot. "Every exercise at the barre helps dancers establish their center of gravity and maintain it as they move out from it," Luckett explains.

Basic barrework begins with pliés—demi-pliés where both heels are on the floor and grandé pliés, which are deep knee bends where the heels rise off the floor. "You wouldn't put your weight on one leg until you've warmed up both," Lupe Serrano explains. Pliés strengthen the thigh muscles, loosen up the hip joints essential to turnout, and build the abdominal muscles. Most ballet classes will progress through pliés in all five of the basic positions.

Next come a variety of movements such as tendus and ronde de jambe that extend the working leg away from the body's center, while the supporting leg remains straight and stationary. These extensions are low, some just brushing the floor and others, described as dégagés or disengaged, raised slightly above it. Serrano points out that you need to start with low extensions and control them before moving on to positions that require higher extensions.

Movements like ronds de jambe à terre, in which the working leg with the toe pointed and on the floor circles the body from front to back, define the sphere around the dancer's body. Posture plays as critical a role in correctly executing this movement as dancers circle the foot in time to the music. "You jeopardize your relationship to your center, to gravity itself, if your alignment falls apart," Luckett cautions. Teachers will often give posture corrections during this phase of class to help dancers tuck in and straighten up before going on to more complicated movements.

Advice on breathing also may be offered, especially during slow, or adagio, barrework. Striving for control, inexperienced dancers may unconsciously hold their breath when they are performing a step, rather than taking advantage of natural pauses in the music to inhale. "A dancer's breathing also needs to come from the core," Luckett says. "Holding your breath will create tension in the body and inhibit the free flow of movement. Breathing has a rhythmic component and the movement needs to be aligned with it."

Gradually the class moves on to exercises such as grands battements, or high kicks, with the working leg held straight. These require high extensions that the body is sufficiently limber to achieve after 25 minutes of barrework. Teachers will vary the pace of barrework to refresh dancers' muscle memory. It is also a way to prepare the dancers for the complex rhythmic variations that the choreography they learn and perform will require. Most critically, however, the changing pace—the adagio (slow) and the allegro (fast)—takes the dancers through a full warmup before they begin to move across the floor. "You need slow and fast movement before you're ready to go to the center," says Serrano. "Adagio requires control and allegro requires syncopation."

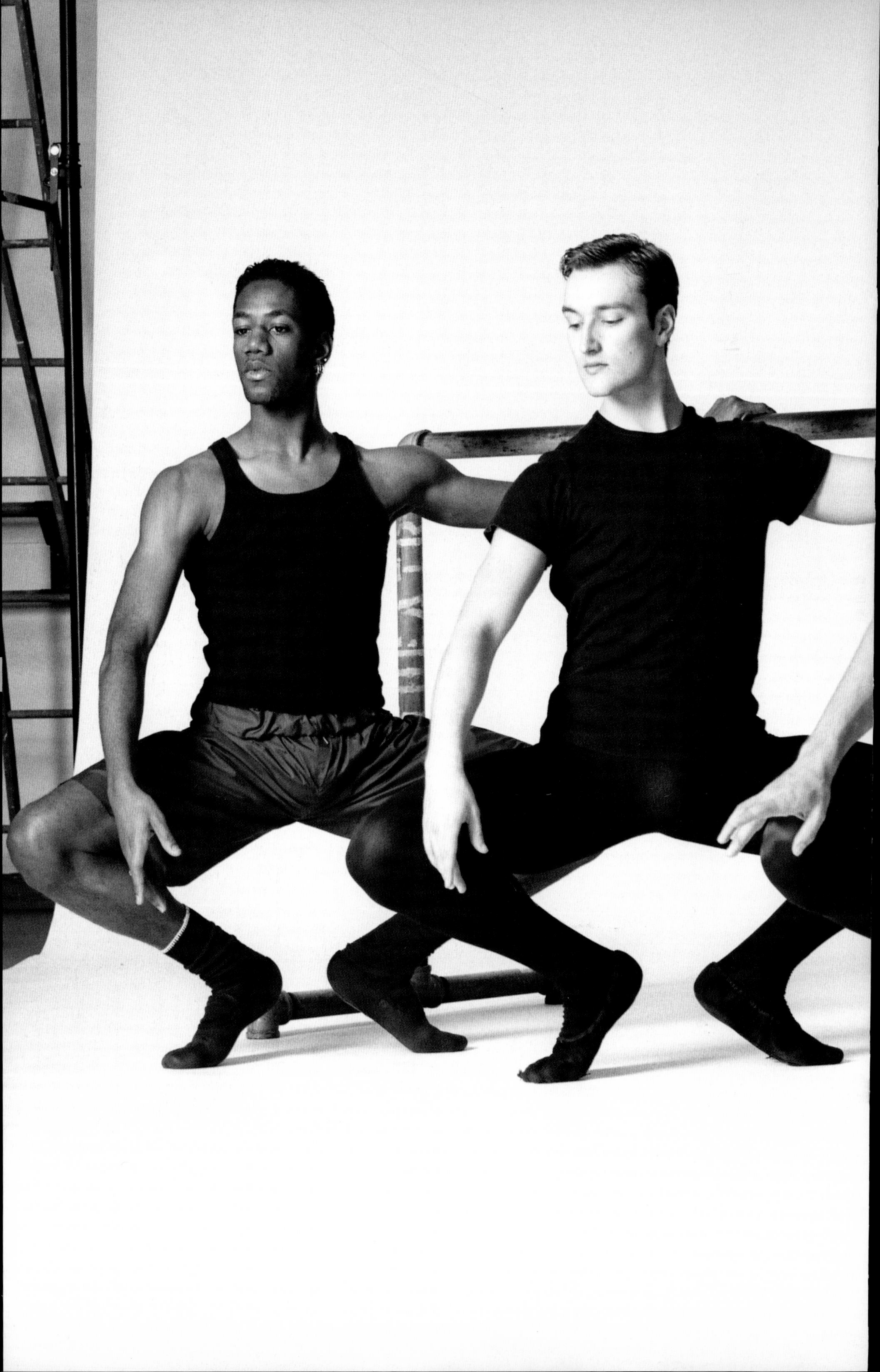

In class, a fully executed position is the goal. From the tip of a toe pointed in a tendu to the tilt of a head to fingers extended in a stylized port de bras, the dancer's body should form one long, unbroken line. Unless, of course, there's a distraction. Here corps de ballet members (dog excepted), work on articulating a position's shape.

69

Performing a sequence from *Etudes*, a neoclassical ballet choreographed by Harold Lander, members of the corps de ballet run through barrework on pointe. Pointe class, which lasts about an hour, usually begins at ten or eleven years old for students who are interested and have advanced to a level where the muscles in their feet and legs have developed enough strength to sustain them. When a dancer becomes a professional, she no longer takes a separate class to refine her pointe tech-

CE

The work at the center begins at first adagio—slowly. Dancers will develop a position such as an arabesque, left, and hold it for several beats. It's a way of building balance, but also of refining details. Here corps members Marta Rodriguez Coca and Jennifer Alexander hold their arms in fifth position to emphasize the torso's verticality in contrast to the extended leg. This stage of center work offers an opportunity to carefully perfect positions, stretching a leg to greater heights, nudging turnout a little farther, checking the mirror for a tucked-in chin.

While teachers will ask dancers to perform simple combinations of steps at the barre, the challenge of creating an unbroken flow of movement happens in the center. This part of class usually begins with about ten minutes of adagio work, a series of slowly developed positions that melt into one another and build up the dancers' control. "Adagio helps dancers to develop the strength to sustain the large poses of classical ballet," says Clinton Luckett. "You must be able to create a shape and then hold it."

This work of sustaining movement involves taking exercises done earlier at the barre to another level, one where there is no longer an actual physical support, and the dancers' sense of their center becomes their sole stabilizing force. Here a simple leg position done at the barre, such as a passé, becomes something more—the essential preparation for a pirouette. The foot of the working leg, which is completely turned out, is pointed and slowly raised up to the knee, and all it takes to revolve is one downward, centrifugal thrust of the supporting leg.

One way to think about this part of class is to see it as the third dimension of ballet, the point at which the rectilinear positions performed at the barre break free of the grid and start to move through space. The upper body becomes a focus. Positions of the head and shoulders are called épaulement, which literally means "shouldering." As dancers move through a series of positions in the center, one shoulder thrusts ahead on the diagonal as the other goes backwards, making for a dynamic, graceful plunge forward through space. The steps in a ballet combination need to be just as fluid as someone walking across a room.

Soon the pace picks up, and the dancers begin to travel across the floor more swiftly. The teacher makes up each combination on the spot, adjusting them according to what he or she has observed the dancers need. Sequences may involve turns—pirouettes, fouettés, piqué turns—and basic linking steps such as pas de chat.

There are two categories of turns, en dedans, or "inside," and en dehors, or "outside." Multiple turns in either direction are an increasingly popular feat for ballerinas and bravura male dancers, and combinations may be set to give dancers a chance to try them in the safety of the studio. Some dancers find it easier to maintain their sense of balance than others, but spotting is critical for everyone. It's common to see dancers line up again and again to perform a combination. "You only get one shot in a performance," reminds Luckett. "You never really can attain perfection. You always want one more try, and class is the place to keep that momentum going."

"Adagio helps dancers to develop the strength to sustain the large poses of classical ballet. You must be able to create a shape and hold it, and create an unbroken line of movement flowing from one position into the next."

Ballet master Guillaume Graffin gives corrections to corps members practicing tendus front and back (top row). The goal is an unbroken line, even when only one leg is bearing the body's entire weight. Dancers (bottom left) with the working leg in passé, or retiré, and preparing in fourth position (bottom right) to execute a pirouette. Next page: corps de ballet members Adrianne Schulte, David Hallberg, and Angela Snow hold a passé; row at left, members of corps hold positions to build balance and control. Once in the center, dancers face the mirror so they can correct themselves.

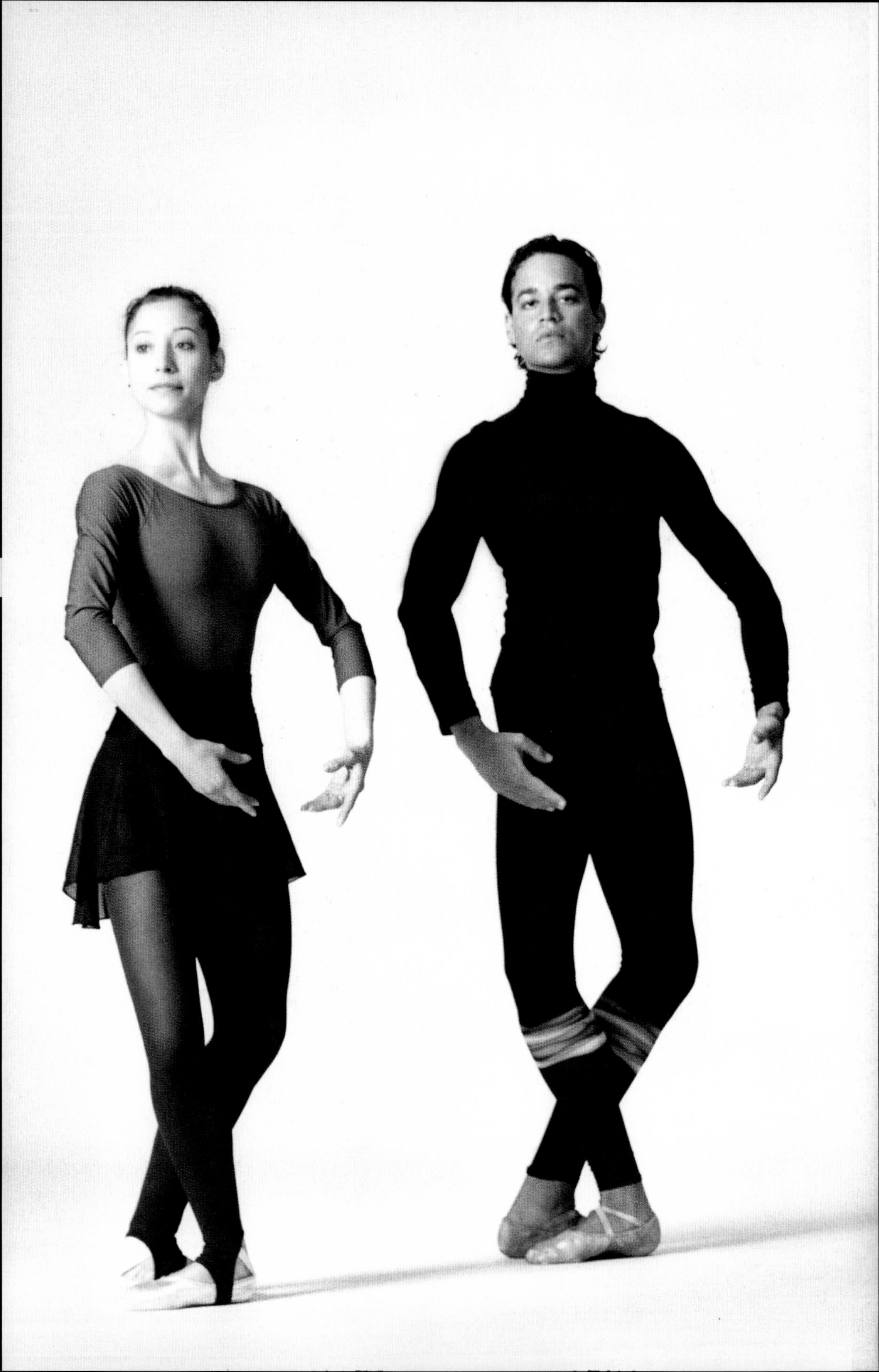

After the adagio portion of center-work comes faster combinations that include jumps in place and across the floor. Preparing for a jump begins with a plié, far left, which helps the dancer gain greater elevation. Here corps members Erica Cornejo and Ricardo Torres perform soubresauts, petit allegro jumps that begin in fifth position, take off, and land cleanly in the same position. As jumps become larger and cover ground, a dancer's extension and line are as important as the jump's height. On page 85. Gennadi Saveliev, top left, and Carlos Lopez and Julio Bragado-Young, right, perform cabrioles. On page 87, Lopez peforms a sissonne split.

Ballet aspires to defy gravity, to create an airborne lightness, and jumps play a critical role in that. (In an interesting historical footnote, jumping entered the ballet vocabulary later than most of the steps: it was an eighteenth-century innovation that allowed ballerinas to show their agility and more of their legs.) The last 15 minutes of every class takes dancers through a series of combinations that improve their jumps and, just as important, their landings. Even the very youngest ballet students will perform skipping and hopping dances at the end of each class, early preparation for the jumps they will learn when they are older.

There are two types of jumps, petit, or little allegro, and grand, or big, allegro. They require slightly different skills. Petit allegro work needs quickness and musicality, while grand allegro needs power and control. "You take the form you've built through classwork literally to another level," explains Clinton Luckett. "Grand allegro explodes your adagio into the air."

Another way to classify jumps breaks them down to their mechanics: jumps from two feet to two feet, such as a soubresaut; from two feet to one foot, such as a sissone; from one foot to two feet such as a tombé assemblé; or from one foot to the other, such as a grand jète. A teacher will demonstrate a step as well as say it, but by putting it in one of these groups, a beginner may learn it more easily.

Jumps vary, but the fundamental aerodynamics stay the same. Every jump originates in a plié, a bend at the knees that thrusts up to a relevé that leaves the floor; a petit allegro jump begins with a shallower bend, a grand allegro jump with a deeper one. Some jumps are stationary, like the rapid footwork known as changement, where the feet change front to back in fifth position while the dancer is in the air. This batterie of steps, which famously occurs in Act II of *Giselle*, is a test of a ballerina's skill, control, and speed. Other jumps travel, creating a chain of movement, such as jeté-jeté–assemblé. "Jumps don't happen in isolation," notes Luckett. "You need to initiate the momentum for them, usually with little refined steps that are like a running start."

Men and women perform different jumps in classical ballet, with the most dramatic grand allegro ones, those that turn in the air, reserved for male dancers. "Men have the power in their hamstrings, buttocks, and calves to propel themselves and stay suspended up there long enough to turn," Luckett says. While jumping demands a degree of athleticism on the part of female as well as male dancers, its effect goes beyond sheer physical prowess. "Ballet is about a high feeling in the body. It isn't earthly—it's refined, elevated, it moves upward. That's the impetus behind jumping," Luckett says. "It energizes the dancer's entire body."

"Petit and grand allegro work requires speed, dynamism, and precision. Jumps don't happen in isolation. You need to initiate the momentum for them."

89

Far left: the jumping ends in a burst of energy with dancers vying with one another for greater height and dramatic style. At the end of class, near left, members of the corps de ballet always applaud the teacher. "The etiquette at the end is reverence," notes Kevin McKenzie. "That meant you bowed to or curtsied to the teacher and to the accompanist. Now students prefer to applaud. We do it because it's an acknowledgment of the teacher's cumulative knowledge, of what they give to us. Ballet is still passed on orally, generation to generation, and the teacher represents that entire history."

REHE

PERFECTING
THE ART

or professional dancers, the hardest work takes place in rehearsal, in rigorous coaching sessions in which ballet masters critique every aspect of a performance-in-the-making. The hours spent in the studio are the real test of a dancer's dedication and artistic ability. It means patiently repeating passages while a coach hones every step. And for some, it's the springboard to creating a distinctive interpretation of a role.

Ballet masters usually work one-on-one with soloists and principal dancers. It is one of the privileges of graduating from the corps de ballet to the higher ranks. Coaching allows a dancer to stretch beyond the limits of classwork and group rehearsal, to address particular problems and smooth out persisting flaws. "A good coach will be honest and tell you how to make it better within your particular gifts and limitations. They help you find your natural coordination," says principal dancer Gillian Murphy.

Each dancer needs to focus on a different aspect of his or her performance. "You have to get to know them," says ballet mistress Georgina Parkinson, formerly a ballerina with England's Royal Ballet. "Dancers speak entirely with their bodies. What they say needs color, energy, and rhythm." It's part of a coach's function to help a dancer shade a performance. Good coaching may help a soloist with potential make the leap to principal; even top-ranked dancers rely on the process to keep them polished. "I've always had pretty strict coaches and I think you need that discipline," says Marcelo Gomes, who was recently named to principal from the soloist ranks.

Sometimes a principal dancer may turn to a coach to help him or her over the hurdles of a particular role, or to find a deeper meaning or greater purity in their interpretations. The coaches, or ballet masters, usually are former principal dancers themselves. Teaching the next generation is part of giving back to the art of ballet, another instance of ballet's dependence on oral tradition.

When coaching, ballet masters focus on a constellation of qualities that are prized in dance. When someone is said to have "a beautiful line," or "great classicism," it means they take these qualities to an extraordinary level. Some key qualities pictured in the following pages are:

LINE
This may be the single most important aspect of a dancer's presentation. It means that a dancer's body expresses a position cleanly and fully. There's a sense the entire gesture stretches out to an imaginary horizon and the entire body is aligned within that gesture. Nothing pokes out in an odd or awkward way, interrupting the movement's natural flow. Instead, the body seems to make a clean, unbroken movement, organic and perfect.

ELEVATION
The height of a jump can transform a straightforward series of steps into a heart-stopping burst of energy. Audiences thrill to huge, ground-clearing elevation, but

maintaining the correct position in mid-air amplifies the impact of the jump's height.

PURITY

This quality means that a movement is executed cleanly, without any sloppiness. Nothing is flying out of alignment, nothing affected or excessive has been added. "I hate to see a messy step. It's like a pianist in a concert. If the notes aren't right and clear, you won't listen" says Irina Kolpakova, a former prima ballerina with the Kirov Ballet and now an ABT coach.

MUSICALITY

Ballet is performed to music; the score and the choreography are fundamentally intertwined. Dancers need to phrase their steps to the music, not merely keep time. That means more than finishing on the beat. A dancer must embody the music's internal rhythms, with his or her steps accenting the notes and vice versa.

Other qualities that can shade a performance and give it character and tone include:

DELICACY

Not every role calls for the most feminine of qualities, but in those that do, this is where details count—how a dancer holds her hands, for instance, not letting her wrists hang limp but maintaining the position right through to her fingertips. Delicacy demands a graceful presentation, one that creates a sense of airiness and weightlessness.

EXPRESSIVENESS

Dancers must use their bodies as well as their faces to convey the choreography's emotional content. An audience can read an eloquent back or yearning arms as well as an expressive face. Dancers must use all the aspects of performance at their command, from their eyes to their hands to how they stand, to shade movement and give it meaning.

AMPLITUDE

It means expressing a position to its very fullest, from the curve of an arm to the arch of a foot. Even simple movements can be generous, imbued with what ballet master Kirk Peterson describes as "a sense of giving the movement to the audience, of allowing your heart to extend beyond your fingertips."

DYNAMISM

Infusing movement with energy makes it exciting to watch. When a performer tackles steps with adrenaline, it transforms them into something exciting and dramatic, charging the space and the movement with propulsive purpose.

Dance
day to
line. A
is like a
music
stron
right, yo
ten,

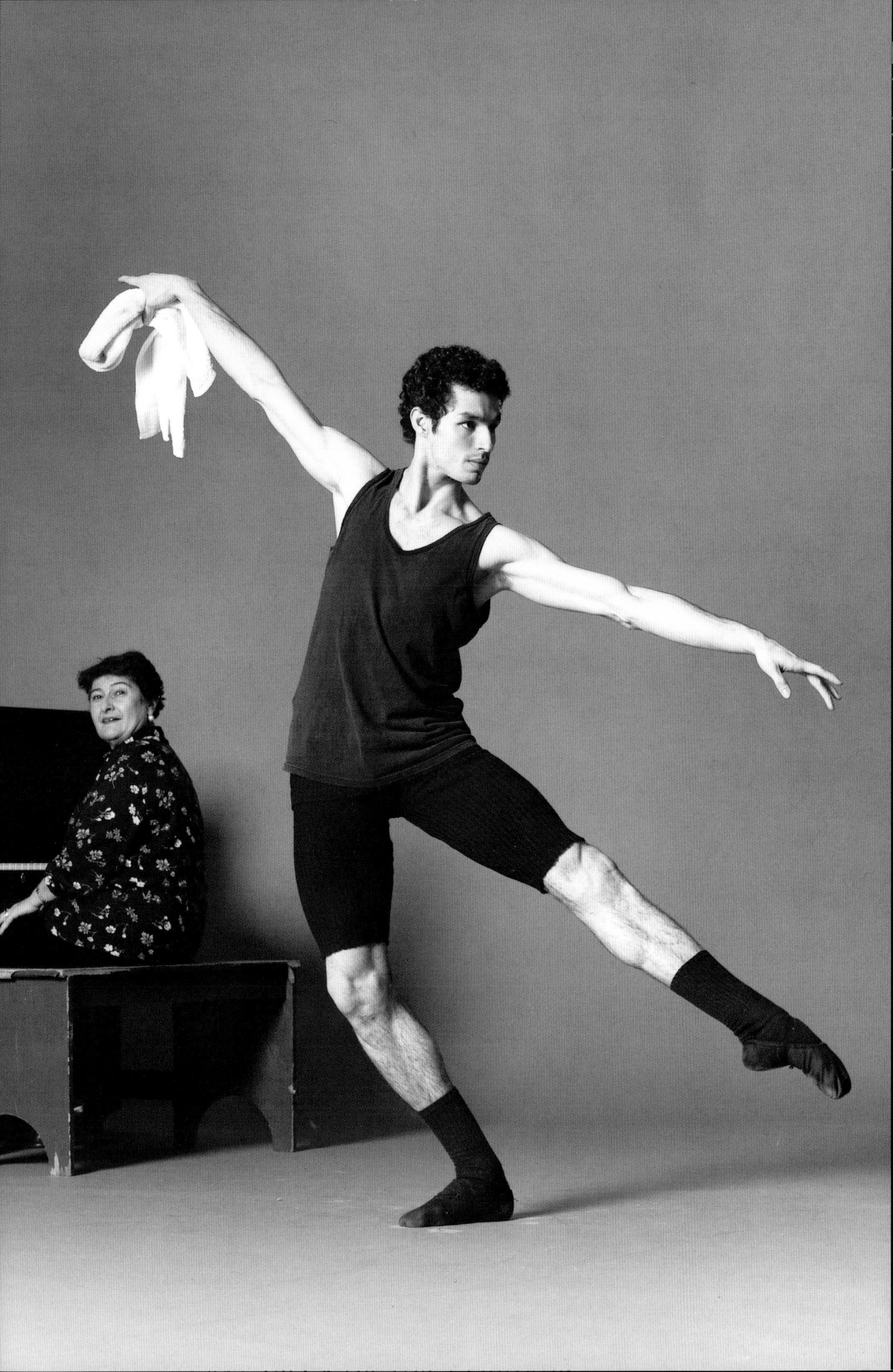

The thrill when a dancer achieves great height lies in the combination of exuberance and control.

Purity and consistency go hand in hand. Here, soloist Herman Cornejo executes five identical jumps.

Keeping time is not
enough. Ballet is not
gymnastics. If there's
no music in your
movement, you have
only a sport.

109

Dancers' bodies are
their voices. They
must convey emotion
physically with bold
power or subtle elo-
quence as the role
demands.

Dancers give their movement to the audience. By offering
the fullest breadth of a movement, the gift becomes
greater. Here, Irina Kolpakova coaches soloist Michelle
Wiles as ABT donor Dr. Joan Kedziora watches.

Movement is ordinary until
it is danced. Dynamism is
the explosive power that the
dancer finds within it.

STAGING A BALLET

The rehearsal process begins in the studio and ends up on stage with costume, orchestra, scenery, and lighting. Principals and soloists often begin work on variations or pas de deux months before they dance a role, snatching a half-hour here or there with their coaches. The corps de ballet dancers will begin learning their parts about three weeks before the curtain goes up, often while they are dancing another ballet at night.

Years of training go into juggling the simultaneous demands of learning and performing. Nearly all the dancers' work takes place in the studio, culminating in a process that is sometimes called "blocking," which puts the whole cast together. At the end, and it may be only the day before, the rehearsals move to the stage, where the dancers have an opportunity to space out their steps. Finally, there's a dress, or tech, rehearsal that brings all the elements and the entire cast together.

The dancers rehearse separately, with the principals in one studio, the soloists in another, and the corps de ballet in a third, for maximum efficiency. There's no time in the schedule for the corps de ballet to sit and watch while a principal grapples with a tricky solo. "There are only six or seven rehearsal hours in a day and we might be preparing several full-length productions," says Victor Barbee. "The girls who dance the harlots in *Romeo and Juliet* can be learning the Shades scene in *La Bayadère* while one of the Romeos is in a studio learning his ballroom variation."

A visitor may not notice at first, but in professional dance studios there's a line painted down the center that's identical to the one that dancers find—or sometimes must draw mentally—on the stage. The dancers must gauge their placement in relation to this centerline. Often there are quarterlines as well, dividing the studio floor and ultimately the stage into a kind of grid, similar to the lines on a basketball court, that becomes second nature for the dancers. It's an essential tool for meshing the performances of principals, soloists, and corps.

Eventually, everyone ends up together in a studio for a run-through, but the schedule may allow only one act to be rehearsed at a time. "You try to fix what you can," says Barbee, "but it's only cost-efficient to correct a couple of things when everyone's sitting around." It's at this point that the differences between the depth of the studio and the depth of the stage are addressed. Dancers may be told to spread out more when they reach the stage or to cross downstage "left over right" if large groups on opposites sides must switch places. They have an opportunity to place themselves "on quarter," in relation to the other dancers, and often this is the point at which logistical issues get solved.

SPACING

A spacing rehearsal is a stripped-down run-through of a ballet. Usually there are only work lights on stage, and the dancers simply mark their steps. A ballet that typically runs two hours in performance may take only an hour to space.

The function of spacing is to acquaint the dancers with the stage and the wings, which will vary depending on the theater. Shallow wings can mean adjusting entrances or exits, especially if a dancer must leap into or out of them. A spacing rehearsal also allows dancers to orient themselves in terms of the set—if the set is up—so that they can modulate their movements to use the space established as the ballet's framework. Sometimes dancers may review a ballet's spacing while the set of a previous ballet has yet to be struck, or taken down. Some dancers also use the spacing rehearsal as an opportunity to move through the stage space in their costumes. It gives them a little more familiarity with the way it will feel when they actually perform.

TECH/DRESS REHEARSAL

A technical or dress rehearsal will take place with the sets, lighting and a full orchestra, but rarely does one pair of dancers have the opportunity to perform the entire ballet. Instead, time and costs dictate that the principal casts alternate acts, each getting to dance one act with all the accoutrements of a live performance. It is a reflection of the dancers' ability and experience that they can glean the information they need from this.

While this rehearsal is run as much as possible like a performance, Barbee says that this is usually the point at which the dancers discover a door that they had rehearsed as opening out actually opens in—meaning an entrance will take longer than planned—or a hundred other problems will crop up. It is also the last moment for adjusting the whole scene. "Something may look fine in the studio, and on stage you need to tweak it," he says. "We work with a live canvas and you want to make sure it has a focus."

THE MUSIC

During the tech/dress rehearsal, the conductor may stop from time to time and ask the leading dancer about the tempo if he hasn't had the opportunity to see them rehearse the role in the studio. This is more than a courtesy. A conductor for a ballet company's orchestra needs to strike a balance between accommodation and collaboration. ABT usually performs at the Metropolitan Opera House in New York with an orchestra of seventy, but the constraints on rehearsal time are considerable. The conductor must have a clear idea where the biggest challenges of the performance will lie. "He or she needs to know the steps as well

as the dancers do," says Susan Jaffe. When the moment comes, the conductor must gauge exactly how much a phrase can be stretched out or speeded up to establish an appropriate pace for the dancer—without undermining the musical structure.

A conductor learns which ballerinas take their fouettés fast, which dancers have a big jump and need the beat slower to accommodate the time in the air, who likes a little extra time to hold and show a position. "There are so many different ways to interpret a phrase," says Jaffe. "You can hang behind a phrase, which many lyrical dancers do. You can anticipate the beat and when it comes, it's almost underscoring your movement. It's not just a matter of the right steps; it's becoming the music in movement."

THE COSTUMES

How many costumes are used in a full-length ballet? 100? 200? 250? Not counting headwear or shoes, *Coppélia* uses 100, *La Bayadère*, 200, and *The Sleeping Beauty* ties with *Le Corsaire* at 250 costumes.

Like many large companies, ABT's wardrobe maintains thousands of costumes. Since they are even more expensive to produce than to refurbish, many are used generation after generation until the production is completely redone. Carla Fracci's costume for Act I of *Giselle* is still worn by various principals, and Angel Corella now uses some of Mikhail Baryshnikov's costumes. When a costume is refitted on a principal, his or her name is simply added to an inside seam alongside the names of the other dancers who have worn it before. No one's name is ever crossed out.

Ballet costumes pose special challenges to designers. They must fit skintight yet have complete mobility. "We use a lot of strategic panels of stretch fabrics," says wardrobe supervisor Bruce Horowitz. These get tucked under arms and hidden beneath seams where the audience won't see them. Corset-like, form-fitting tutus have another hidden solution: several different rows of hooks in back so they can be fastened to accommodate different-size ribcages.

THE MAKEUP

Large companies have makeup artists to help the dancers get ready for a performance, but many ballerinas like to do their own. "Every ballerina is very picky about it. It's so important that she feel beautiful. If she doesn't, her performance will suffer," says Jaffe. There are some old conventions in ballet makeup, such as heavy swept-up eyebrows that give an exotic, cat-like look, which

some makeup artists still use. Jaffe always preferred a more natural look, often not making up her eyebrows at all. She also adjusted her makeup according to her character. When she was cast as Lizzie Borden in *Fall River Legend*, she remembers that she wanted to look as plain as possible. "I wore brown lipstick, I didn't wear any rouge, I made my face pale," Jaffe remembers. "I felt Lizzie and I knew her. I wanted to look like her as much as possible."

Ballerinas also have latitude about how they arrange their hair, providing they remain in character. A ballerina can decide where her Juliet will wear her pearls, how high she will have her hair up in the first act of *Giselle* and other details that will not change the overall effect of the character's costuming, but will become part of that ballerina's interpretation.

CHOREO

MAKING THE DANCE

Ballet has a distinct vocabulary, but it's the choreographer who takes music and dancers and makes it speak. Marius Petipa took the arabesque and made it the essence of the Swan Queen's choreography in *Swan Lake*. Odette's anguished pose, one leg extended, her arms flowing back like wings, elevates a standard classroom position to a stirring image of beauty and grief.

WATCHING THE DANCE

Choreography by definition creates a chain of steps, a flow of movement that covers space in time to music. Contemporary ballet choreography often uses a particular piece of music as the de facto subject as well as the score of a piece.

When a ballet tells a story, even indirectly, the choreography has a less abstract purpose. The corps de ballet members waltzing in Act II of *Swan Lake* are not simply girls in tutus but Odette's enchanted entourage, with fluttering arms and arched necks echoing her signature steps. They serve as a visual leitmotif.

Without narrative, the music becomes the movement's propulsive force. For the audience watching and listening, the ballet's meaning may not reveal itself in literal images. Like a Jackson Pollock painting, a ballet may be about movement and music itself.

While it's facile to say that ballet, like all art, comes down to personal taste, there's an element of truth to that. Still, there are a few criteria to keep in mind whether a ballet is classical or contemporary, narrative or pure dance:

Does a choreographer use the classical vocabulary creatively? A dance made on ballet-trained bodies that involves pointework isn't necessarily good ballet. A choreographer using the classical medium must do so with a purpose—because it amplifies or underscores the movements, because it complements or articulates the music, because it is suitable to his or her theme or story.

Do music and movement belong together? Using music from a certain period does not determine the movement vocabulary. Wonderful ballets have been made to works by avant-garde composer Philip Glass, and brilliant modern dances pieces have been made to Bach, but audiences can sense either a synergy or a disconnect between movement and music.

Does the choreography have a vision propelling it? Again, the answer is subjective. One viewer may be moved, another bored. Yet even choreographers like George Balanchine, who refused to tie works to one meaning or another, had the keenest sense of the human condition. In the hands of masters, ballet's highly codified vocabulary will tell the greatest truths of human nature and the human heart, and the audience will recognize them.

THE DANCERS' ROLE

When a ballet is created, or "made," on a dancer, he or she instantly becomes an indelible part of its history. It is a ballet tradition to acknowledge a role's original interpreter, and often program notes will name them, even if a ballet is one hundred years old. This practice may have evolved because the process of making a ballet involves a great deal of collaboration.

Dancers relish this chance to be seen in a fresh light. Working with a choreographer is a break from the routine of perfecting technique and interpretation. "I get into the studio and I try to make visible what's in the choreographer's mind," says principal dancer Angel Corella. "Sometimes a choreographer wants you to have an idea, and sometimes you are the idea." That happened when Stanton Welch created a solo for Corella at the beginning of *Within You, Without You*, a work featuring several choreographers and the music of George Harrison that premiered in 2003. "Every step felt personal," recalls Corella. "It was the first time someone made a solo for me, and it speaks about who I am. Stanton wanted me to seem very normal, as though I were dancing around my apartment." The steps, to the song "Something," are muscular and expressive. With Corella's casual, disarming style in mind, Welch had him finish the solo by scratching his back.

Many dancers feel they are the choreographer's instruments. "You have to be willing not to make the ballet about you," says principal dancer Julie Kent. "You remove yourself from the equation and go in the choreographer's direction." While the process can be slow, it can mean your body becomes the canvas, as Kent found when she worked with Nacho Duato on *Without Words* (see "Collaboration"). "With some choreographers, each step is a birth and you do it over and over until the next step comes to them. It's very reflective of you because your body helps shape it," she says.

Some choreographers have a clear idea before they go into the studio. Former principal dancer Susan Jaffe worked with Twyla Tharp on several pieces and found Tharp had most of the steps worked out before she began rehearsing. "Twyla's not dogmatic but she knows what she wants," says Jaffe. "If you can't mimic a combination she shows you, she'll look at what you can do and if she likes it, she'll keep it." Since Tharp's choreography often works in counterpoint to the music, she has dancers count out the beats for their entrances. "Twyla would tell me to start counting from the point when the other dancers began a certain move, and then come in after 50 beats," says Jaffe. Keeping track of the beat means never losing focus and concentration.

THE CHOREOGRAPHER'S CHALLENGE

Every choreographer confronts the same problems. What is the mission he or she has been asked to fulfill—make a ballet to music by George Harrison or by Richard Rodgers? What kind of ballet? An "opening" ballet, an easy piece that leads off a program? A "closing" ballet that sends the audience out in a good mood? Or the lynchpin of the program?

These questions will influence the music that a choreographer selects. "It better be music you love, because you're going to hear it one hundred times," says Wendy Perron, a choreographer and editor at *Dance Magazine* who is working on a solo for former ABT principal Martine van Hamel. Perron may use the music to help to create a structure, if the piece breaks down into distinct sections. The music sets the pace, but the choreographer must decide how to use it. "After you have six dancers on stage for a while, you want to have a solo, or a trio," Perron says, to punctuate the music and the movement.

Most important is finding an idea big enough to fill the music. "You need something that will require detail to fill it in; otherwise you will get tired and so will the audience," Perron says.

WORKING WITH LAR LUBOVITCH

Steps don't exist in a vacuum; choreographers don't enter the studio with a ballet full-blown in their head. To create the movements that will follow one another to become a sequence of steps, a choreographer needs bodies and music.

Each choreographer has his or her own approach to the process. Lar Lubovitch begins with the music. He will listen to a piece until he has it memorized, then sketch out shapes that he hears within it. These shapes do not literally become the steps, but they are a starting point when he goes into the studio. "The music tells me something," he says, "and I try to tell it back."

A recent piece that Lubovitch created for ABT as part of the Richard Rodgers centenary celebrations, "*...smile with my heart*," ends with a pas de deux to the melody of Rodgers and Hart's "My Funny Valentine." Lubovitch made the piece on ABT company members Sandra Brown and Marcelo Gomes. From the start, he had the ballet's final image, with Brown lying insouciantly on the floor, her head in her hand, and Gomes clinging adoringly to her. All he needed was the ballet that would precede it.

Lubovitch felt that the lyrics of the song were a man's reassurance to a woman. He saw Brown as fragile, believing herself unworthy of love at the beginning of the pas de deux. "Vulnerability is immensely powerful as a sexual attractor," he explains. "By the end, she really is in control of the relationship." After many repeats and false starts, the steps to the duet reflected that trajectory. "A movement may feel inevitable to the audience, but that doesn't mean it's clear to you immediately when you're working on it," he says. "Every next move is a bump until you get over it. It's very uncomfortable when nothing exists, and you reach into the air and fill it with someone's body."

While he singles out Brown's passionate dancing as an influence on the ballet, Lubovitch doesn't tell dancers what they should feel in his pieces. "The story I tell is going to be based on what the dancers emanate in the studio, but I always speak in terms of what's required physically. I never talk about the emotion. If you capture the emotion in physical shapes, it's as eloquent as words."

Lubovitch feels deep pleasure when a work has been completed, but he points out it will evolve as it is performed. "No ballet's ever exactly the same twice," he says. "Ballets change hands. We don't really know what *Swan Lake* looked like. A new dancer will take '...*smile with my heart*' somewhere else, and you have to leave room for that."

"I know the ending before I begin. I have to see the destination before I can get there."
-Lar Lubovitch

"I write in movement, but I don't conceive steps according

The dancers are integral to the process and you absorb

to a certain level of technique.

their essence."

"Fear will always be a part of the process for me. Imagine

Even with the water there, you're full of terror mixed with

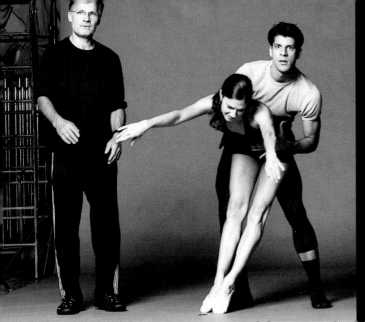

...yourself jumping off a cliff into deep water.

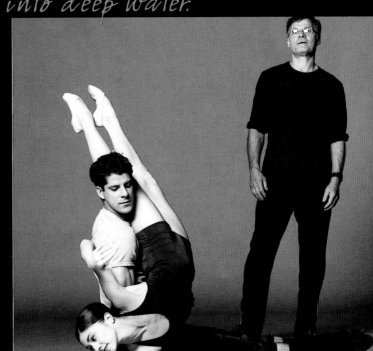

joy."

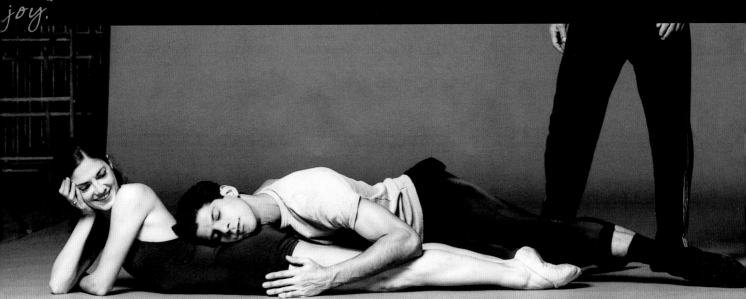

reating a ballet is a process of collaboration that doesn't end in the studio. Costume, lighting, and set designers play their part. The last century saw choreography and staging fuse to such a degree that certain ballets are as identified with their overall look as their choreography. When Serge Diaghilev's Ballets Russes turned to Pablo Picasso and Léon Bakst in the 1920s to work with choreographers like George Balanchine and Michel Fokine and create entire productions, the overall conception of a ballet took on an entirely new dimension.

Today the choreographer rather than an impresario usually develops a piece's staging and conception. When Nacho Duato created *Without Words* for ABT in 1999, he decided on an unusual approach for its staging even before he finished working out the steps. The work would be performed in front of giant photographs of the dancers in their roles. As the ballet progressed, the photographs, projected on scrims, would slowly change, singling out and isolating certain moments.

ABT offered the task of photographing the images to Nancy Ellison. When she went into the studio with Duato and the dancers, he arranged them in several positions, then stepped back and allowed Ellison to pick her angles. "They were like monumental sculptures, and every so often he would rearrange them," she remembers. "I kept moving around them, sometimes just shooting a detail, sometimes the whole ensemble."

Duato didn't ask the dancers to perform the ballet for Ellison, nor did he give it a particular meaning. Ellison discovered when the ballet premiered that he had picked incidental moments for the dancers' poses, rather than climatic ones. "He wanted me to create my own sense of iconic imagery," she says. "I'd shoot a hand or a thigh very erotically, yet in the ballet, it turned out to be ephemeral." The randomness imbued the changing images with the quality of omens or portents. It gave the ever-dissolving, ever-changing backdrop a role in its own right, one signaling the sadness and loss that would envelop the stage in the final image, when a male dancer turns his back to the audience to stare yearningly across a darkened stage at the image of a woman who has gone.

COLLABORATION

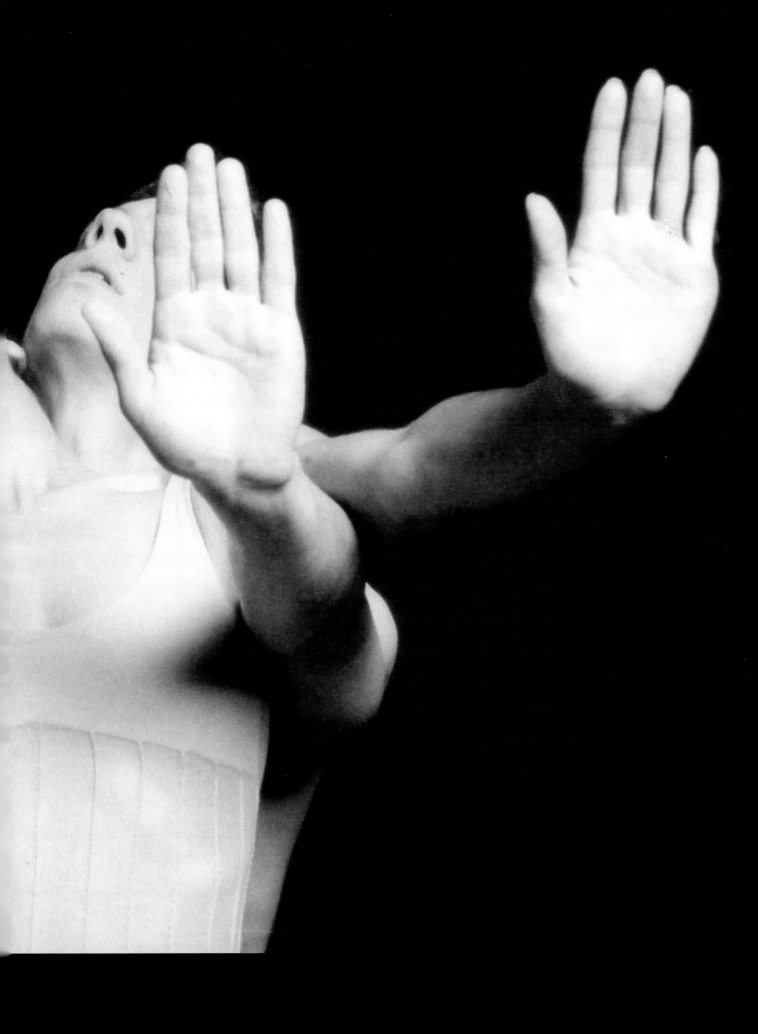

Photo by Paul Kolnik

"Duato didn't want the images to be about the choreography," Ellison says. "He wanted them to have a dramatic impact of their own, to be powerful enough to sustain what was happening on stage, almost like the visual residue of what had just been danced."

Ballet remains an oral tradition handed down from teacher to student, generation after generation. This applies to choreography as well as to the fundamentals of ballet technique. Like the rebellious readers in Ray Bradbury's *Fahrenheit 451* who memorize books in order to preserve them, a dancer will memorize a ballet's roles, becoming in effect a repository for that choreographer's work. Although there are now several forms of dance notation to record and preserve steps, it's still customary for roles to be taught to new dancers by someone who has danced them. Usually the choreographer has selected that dancer; but if the choreographer is no longer alive, sometimes the arrangement will be more informal. A dancer who premiered a major role in a ballet may be tapped when a company wishes to stage that work, and will come to "set" the entire piece on the company.

At a large company like ABT, the ballet masters take responsibility for teaching certain works in the repertory, particularly if they frequently danced the works themselves, or worked with the choreographer when the ballet was created. Often a dancer from outside the company who learned the steps directly from the choreographer will be called in to tighten up the details or to stage works with which the company is unfamiliar.

While debuting in a classic like *The Sleeping Beauty* can be a milestone for a dancer, sometimes stepping into a relatively new ballet can be even more daunting. The dancers on whom the roles were originally made are not only still performing, but even may appear in that particular part during the season. "I try to think of it as something brand-new, instead of second-hand clothing," says Stella Abrera, who learned a featured role in Mark Morris's *Gong* that had been originally made on Nina Ananiashvili and Michele Wiles. A graceful lyrical dancer known for her careful attention to form, Abrera found the part a challenge. "It showed off exciting bravura dancing, lots of huge grands jetés and fast pirouettes, and that took a 110-percent effort," she remembers.

Ballet master Guillaume Graffin taught Abrera the steps. When Morris first choreographed the piece, Graffin went into the studio with him and learned each role, taking extensive notes so that he could stage the ballet for the company in future. There were passages that even he couldn't remember while coaching Abrera, so they turned to the company's private library of videotapes, a subgrade recording of a performance, which the company keeps as a choreographic record. Between Graffin's memory and a grainy video, Abrera finally mastered the difficult solo.

Great ballet partnerships seem rarer on stage than in life. Perhaps that's why those who saw Rudolf Nureyev and Margot Fonteyn still speak of their extraordinary alchemy. In the pantheon of dance partnerships, which is always under debate, but certainly includes Carla Fracci and Erik Bruhn, Cynthia Gregory and Fernando Bujones, Alessandra Ferri and Julio Bocca, the passion and tenderness of the Fonteyn-Nureyev partnership became the paradigm. Their performances had an indelible romantic glow.

While few partnerships become the stuff of legend, many go beyond simply performing a pas de deux correctly. A good partnership makes a more enjoyable performance, for the dancers as well as the audience, and all partnerships, great or not, begin in the studio. "Every partner is different," says Robert Hill, a choreographer and former ABT principal who has danced frequently with ballerina Julie Kent (photo right and following pages). "Some just aren't in it one hundred percent, while with others, it's almost intuitive, you don't even need to talk about what you're doing."

HANDS AND TURNS

Most of the time, the two dancers will start working out the physical kinks first. Even if they've danced other roles together, or each has danced the ballet with another partner, every pas de deux poses fresh obstacles. "Maybe you need to give your partner more time before she starts a pirouette, or step farther back when she jumps into your arms for a lift. Sometimes, you'll do it over and over, and just talk the hell out of a problem," says Hill.

Every ballerina has different preferences as well, like how she likes to turn in a pas de deux, and a partner must learn them. "Some ballerinas just don't like to be handled very much if they are good turners," says Susan Jaffe. The man must help the turn, usually gently pulling the ballerina clockwise toward him with the right hand, while pushing away with the left. If a ballerina has strength and balance, her partner may barely apply any force or direction to his grip. The ballerina on her part must step into the turn at a sufficient distance from her partner so he has room to avoid being kicked. A ballerina may also prefer to phrase a turn a certain way. "You can say, 'Here, at this point, can you bring me around slowly? I want to show my port de bras and end in a deep back bend,'" says Jaffe.

LIFTS AND BALANCES

Some of the most exciting pas de deux choreography involves lifts. Hill notes that the hardest lifts are low ones. For instance, if the ballerina's supporting foot

just brushes the floor while her working leg is extended in arabesque, "it can be really hard on the partner's lower back," says Hill. The high, breathtaking lifts, where the ballerina is held in a pose above her partner's shoulders, are often easier. "Once I get a ballerina above my head, I can stand there all day," he says.

One reason is that most dancers' upper bodies and arms are extremely muscular. While male dancers may not look like they have cultivated body builders' bulging physiques, their biceps are just as strong. When a partner lifts a ballerina above his shoulders, she must yield, or it will become impossible for her partner to complete the position. "You must hold yourself in a controlled, quiet manner and let the man find his center of balance," says Julie Kent. A ballerina helps the lift along by leaping or jumping into her partner's arms, but just as a man must be sensitive to different partners' body types and styles, a woman must also mold her performance to her partner. "A ballerina may have to adjust her takeoff. You can't come at your partner too fast or too slow," says Kent. "The only way to figure it out is by a lot of repeating and effort."

Everyone has a different body, and so a solution with one partner may not work with another. "The nature of movement is such that usually there's more than one way to get there and be true to the choreography," Hill says. Then, once the steps have been mastered, the acting becomes key. "There's nothing worse than someone giving you a reaction that isn't timed right," he notes. For many dancers, eye contact between partners can be essential. "If I can't establish eye contact, I feel lonely," says Jaffe. "The audience will never know, but you can look at somebody and not see them."

In the end, chemistry is chemistry. It can't be summoned; it simply happens. Sometimes two dancers seem to think and move on stage as one. "In the best partnerships," says Hill, "it feels as though you breathe the same breath."

"I've had a great time with my partners in the studio, but you can never create the same energy you get on the stage. That's why it's hard to rehearse a kiss. In the end, you just feel silly."

"The pas de deux is my favorite part of ballet," says Kent. "It's lonely when you're on stage on your own. Performing a pas de deux is like singing a duet with someone, or being part of a chamber orchestra. It's about taking your kinetic energy and his, and moving as one. The biggest challenge comes in the studio. You spend hours there and you really expose yourself. You need someone who will be supportive, and in turn, you need to give at his touch. One person has to decide what's happening, and the way I feel in partnering is that the guy drives the car, and I sit in the back of the convertible with my hair flying the breeze."

Many major ballet companies tour nationally and internationally. For ABT, it's part of the company's mission, dating back to its earliest days under artistic director Lucia Chase. The one-night stands in cities across America may have faded into company lore, but ABT still maintains a schedule that puts the dancers on the road 12 weeks of the year.

For company members, that has rewards and liabilities. "When I joined five years ago, I felt we were going to the ends of the earth," remembers soloist Stella Abrera. "That first year we went to Rio, Korea, and Japan all in a few months. I kept thinking, 'What have I gotten myself into?'" While it sounds glamorous to visit exotic and famous places, most of the time, the dancers are working. "You'd love to pretend you're on vacation, but you have to stay focused," says Abrera. "At most, you have a few hours off. You spend a lot more time at the theater, taking class, rehearsing, and performing. Living out of a suitcase gets old in about a week."

Touring makes tremendous demands not only on the company's artists, but also on the crew. "When we tour domestically, we use a minimum of four semi-tractor-trailers to move the sets, costumes, and lighting," says David Lansky, ABT's production manager. "A big ballet like *Swan Lake* uses eight." Counting the carpenters, electricians, wardrobe mistresses, and other backstage personnel who are essential to mounting the ballets, about 125 people end up on the road. "We're the biggest touring company in the world beside the circus," Lansky notes.

The company brings along its own lighting—some six hundred pieces of equipment—and its own sprung floor, similar to those used on basketball courts, in order to protect the dancers when they are performing on concrete stages where the risk of severe injury is far higher. Often the crew will arrive a day ahead, and work from 8 A.M. to midnight to set up a full-length production before the first performance. While every cast should have an opportunity to become accustomed to variances in the depth of the stage and the wings, often the rehearsal schedule doesn't permit it. "The dancers are incredible. They have the ability to simply adjust," Lansky says. To give them maximum exposure to a new stage, often a dress rehearsal will be split among three casts, with one performing the first act of that night's ballet, another the second, and so on. Somehow, in a way that can seem like a miracle even to Lansky, when the curtain goes up a few hours later, it comes together.

PERF
MAN

OR-

NCE

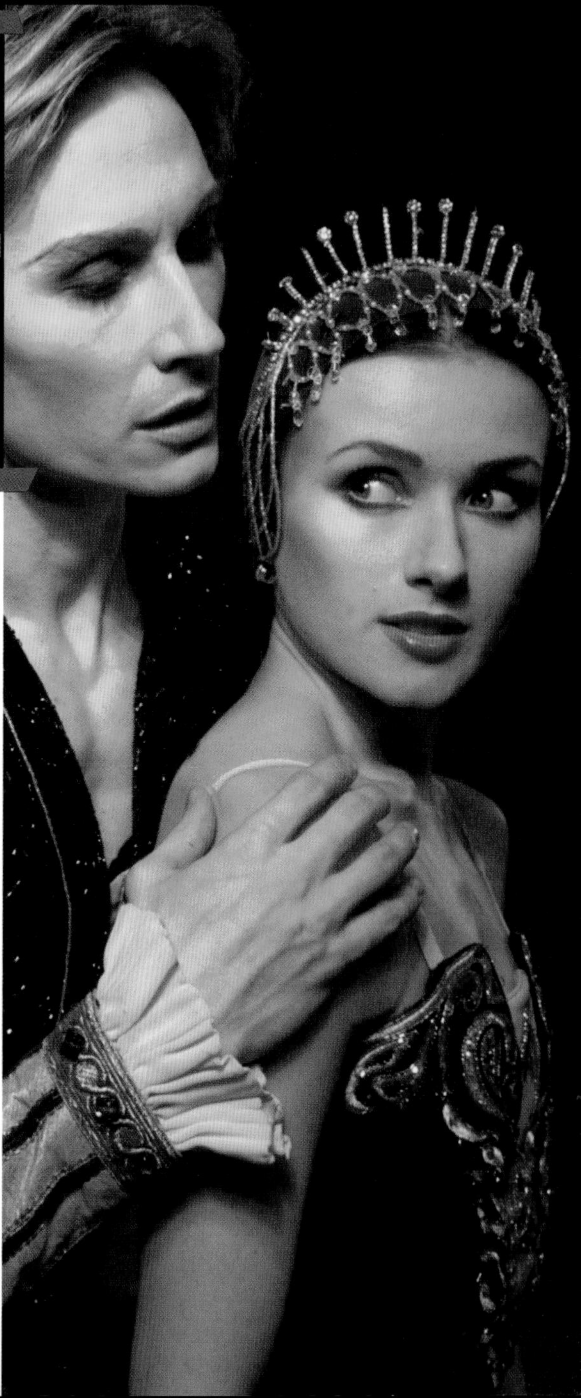

Something happens when the lights dim, the orchestra leader takes his place, and the music starts. A tension sweeps through the audience, a sense of anticipation and longing to lose oneself completely in the performance that's to come.

For dancers, the stage is the ultimate goal, the reason for the hours of class-work, coaching, and rehearsal, the point of striving to master an art form that's arcane and difficult, even for the most gifted. "When people are paying to see you, it's daunting and inspiring," says principal dancer Ethan Stiefel. "Rehearsal and class may be the road to that point, but I'm not going to be remembered for being a great artist in the studio."

In ballet, tradition shapes everyone's performance. Every time a dancer performs the title role of Giselle for the first time, she takes her place in a line stretching back to Carlotta Grisi, the very first to dance the ballet in 1841. That is why ballet companies still alert the press to a dancer's debut in a role, even if the ballet is as frequently performed as *The Nutcracker*. It is a way of acknowledging the heritage that has shaped so many roles.

The struggle to perfect a role is never over. "When you're named a principal, it's the beginning, not the end, of more hard work and intense thinking," says principal dancer Maxim Belotserkovsky. "Our job is endless," agrees his wife and partner Irina Dvorovenko. "You're never done. Every day, every week you must create a new feeling, make your interpretation more fluid. The process of creating never stops—you stop and you're dead."

SIGNATURE ROLES

While principals may dance every ballet that a company gives in a season, most balletgoers pick and choose the casts they want to see. Not every bravura dancer makes a charming Basil in *Don Quixote*, and not every lyrical ballerina can meet the technical demands of Odette/Odile in *Swan Lake*. By the same token, dancers can become famous for their interpretation of a certain role and ticket sales swell each time they perform it.

What identifies a dancer with a role often comes down to the details of his or her interpretation. Dvorovenko has danced Odette/Odile in *Swan Lake* many times and her view of the part is distinctive. She believes that Odette remains enchanted in swan form throughout the ballet, never truly casting off the magician's evil spell even in her tender pas de deux with the prince by the lake. "She's always a swan, the most beautiful, untouchable creature you can imagine," Dvorovenko says. To show Odette's bewitchment, she makes quick, sensitive movements with her arms and neck that echo a swan's fluttering. Dvorovenko also has an expressive back, and in the moment before she succumbs to the magician's summons and tears herself from the prince, her muscles visibly tense. It seems as though her body revolts before yielding to the spell. Hers is a memorable portrayal, although far from the only approach to the role.

CORPS DE BALLET

The corps de ballet creates a human frame for the classical repertory. Without a superbly disciplined ensemble, there can be no *Swan Lake* or *La Bayadère*. The dancers' unity and stylistic consistency plays as essential a role as the ballerina's. "The corps de ballet magnifies the whole performance," says ballet mistress Susan Jones. "They breathe as one, move as one. They must make the same investment as the ballerina."

The corps de ballet emerged in ballet's earliest days, when certain court dances required groups to move in unison as a backdrop to a main couple. By the nineteenth century, the corps de ballet had become a feminine complement to the ballerina, but its geometric potential was not exploited fully until Marius Petipa choreographed *La Bayadère* in the 1870s. It was Petipa who manipulated the corps into kinetic patterns that seemed a visual expression of the music, and who recognized that having 24 identically dressed dancers performing the same steps amplified the choreography in unexpected ways.

The patterns that the corps de ballet must create, whether the ballet is classical or contemporary, requires members to be aware at all times of one another. Jones finds the hardest choice comes when she arranges the order of the dancers—which typically goes from short in front to tall in back. She does not worry about which dancer will lead a row, but which one will come behind her. "I need someone with the ability to understand the bigger picture," Jones says. "The second dancer's placement is critical; the first dancer has no one she follows, but the second must be in synch with the girl right ahead of her and set the form and adhere to it for everyone behind her. It's really a knack."

The corps' uniformity might at a glance resemble the Rockettes, but Jones, a fan of the popular Radio City Music Hall dancers, sees the corps' work as a deeper challenge. "The corps is a living organism," says Jones. "We can get all the girls doing the same thing at the same time, lifting a leg or an arm to the same height, but it's hard to get that movement to have life and juice in it, to make a real contribution to the entire effect."

While it might seem that corps de ballet dancers must sacrifice their individuality, in fact many of the most successful dancers begin in the corps. Jones pays close attention in class to those making an extra effort, and she watches from the audience to see which dancer brings brio and strength to her performance. When someone seems to have potential, she may be cast in what's called a "demi-soloist" role, a variation that gives the dancer an opportunity to shine on her own, polish her performance skills and nudge her technique to a higher level. Ballet aficionados love to scan the corps looking for future stars, and when a corps dancer is given one of the demi-soloist opportunities, the scrutiny intensifies. Whether or not they graduate to soloist rank, Jones' goal is to help the corps members understand their importance despite their relative anonymity. "They must invest themselves artistically. If there's one disgruntled girl, it shows."

STAGE FRIGHT

While at times it's hard to believe the airborne, graceful dancers who glide with little effort through the most intricate choreography are even human, they suffer from the same anxieties and worries as other performers. Some dancers conquer their stage fright with experience, but for others it's simply integral to the experience of performing. "My most nervous moment is always my first entrance," says Dvorovenko. "My heart is popping when I go on. People who don't get nervous don't care." Some dancers even feel nerves are a plus. "It can work toward your performance," says principal dancer Marcelo Gomes. "If you're too calm, you may not get the adrenaline you need to pump you up."

DANCING FOR THE AUDIENCE

No matter how often they dance a part, few dancers ever forget the audience watching in the darkness. "It always takes two," says Gillian Murphy, a dancer recently named to principal rank. "There's the speaker and the listener, you and the audience. You've worked long hours and it comes down to that moment, that performance. The goal isn't just to improve yourself, but to transport people."

Dancers feel the audience as more than a faceless presence. "I want to take people with me for an hour or two," says Belotserkovsky. "I want to say, 'We'll go to my palace, we'll meet my mother, my servants.' When you step on stage, you're the host. You should welcome everyone." He's very aware of applause or silence, and finds his performance responding to it. "It's like a boomerang. I need the audience. I can't do without it."

And for some, the sheer joy of performing has been what's always mattered. "The audience is why I'm a dancer," says Angel Corella. "It makes me happy if I can make other people happy. Our job as dancers isn't very important. We aren't doctors. But if we can make people forget their worries for even a few hours, that's something."

PREPARING

Ballerina Nina
Ananiashvili crafts
every performance
with care. No detail
is left to chance.
She even makes the
hairpieces for cer-
tain roles herself.
"I like to have every-
thing be my own,"
she says. "When I
know all is in order,
I feel more secure."

All dancers have a set routine that they follow before going on stage. This helps them to muster the technique and artistry that an audience expects. It may be something as personal and quirky as eating a steak and having a double espresso beforehand, as Angel Corella admits he likes to do before he dances, or something as soothing and ordinary as taking a nap. For principal dancer Nina Ananiashvili, the ritual begins the day before. She spends the night prior to a performance at home, doing simple tasks like sewing her pointe shoes, reading, and eating dinner with her husband. "I won't accept an invitation, even to see friends. I want to save all of my emotion for the next night," she says.

The morning of the performance, she takes class with the company, has a bite to eat, then spends the afternoon quietly. Two-and-a-half hours before the curtain, she goes to the theater. She checks her costumes to make sure everything is in order. If a hem is torn or a bit of trim is coming off, she'll sew it on herself, anxious to be sure that it's all perfect. She puts on her makeup and arranges her hair, then goes to warm up at the barre near the stage for a half-hour. Next she puts on her first-act costume. At this point, she admits, "My nerves are tingling." Then she goes to check the stage for her first entrance, to be certain, for example, that a door she must go through isn't sticking shut. She also checks any props she may need—a tambourine, a fan. "Small things are important. I feel more secure knowing everything's in place," she explains.

She also prepares several pairs of shoes for each performance. "Our pointe shoes are our instruments," she says. "If something's wrong with my feet, all my mind goes there. I usually have six pairs ready. Soft shoes for one act, stiffer shoes for another, stronger shoes for a variation with a lot of turns." Ananiashvili will routinely change her shoes several times backstage, sometimes even within one act, wearing one pair for a solo, then changing to another for a pas de deux.

At the end, she makes a point of taking a bow at each side of the stage. "The audience likes to see you up close. It's only polite," she says. Afterward she sometimes has so much adrenaline that she feels like she could do another performance on the spot. "That night, I can't sleep until 4 A.M.," she admits. "But I feel like a squeezed lemon the next day. There's nothing left. I cannot dance without giving it my all. I dance like it's my last performance every time."

VIRTUOSO DANCER

What makes a dancer exceptional? Is it artistry or technique—or an elusive combination of the two? The question sounds academic, but dancers who were celebrated only a few decades ago rarely had the technical mastery now deemed routine, even in the corps de ballet. A ballerina who performs a mere thirty-two fouettés today without so much as a double or triple pirouette now receives only a polite round of applause.

Ballet's new athleticism appeals to audiences primed to expect pyrotechnical feats. Speed and strength are easy to recognize, but they once were only an element in creating a dancer's celebrity. Fame was achieved according to skill and superiority within certain categories: bravura or noble for men, adagio or allegro for women. These characterized a dancer as fiery or elegant in style, typed them by physique—compact or tall—and in some measure dictated how they were cast. "To see a dancer as bravura or lyrical now is an oversimplification," says Kevin McKenzie. "A rounded artist has all those qualities we mean when we use those terms."

The result is a new breed of dancer, the virtuoso who can do it all. Many forces have fostered the virtuoso's rise. In recent years superstars such as Mikhail Baryshnikov and Sylvie Guillem shaped audience's expectations to such a degree that anyone who performs certain roles, whether it's Basil in *Don Quixote* or Odette/Odile in *Swan Lake*, will be expected to astonish in technical terms. The American approach to training and performance has helped the trend as well. Companies here don't tend to type dancers early on, while many European schools still train students differently according to their innate strengths.

The more democratic approach has its drawbacks. When a company casts a dancer against type, it may offer a fresh perspective on a role and reveal a dancer's unexpected strengths. Still, a certain blurriness can creep in, obscuring the choreography's details. Once upon a time, a charming soubrette didn't ever have an opportunity to dance the role of the Swan Queen. No more. "Dancers here tend to be more versatile," says ballet master Kirk Petersen. "While your body type certainly will define you to a degree, it all should be part of your package."

If you can do it all, does that mean you can do it all well? Whether a dancer surpasses one rival in technical terms, or falls behind another, as principal dancer Maxim Belotserkovsky puts it, "you still need to leave a mark that's your own." All dancers have their strengths and weaknesses. While they may be prized for their virtuosity, they always will be loved for what they do best.

Breathtaking. Sensational. Thrilling. All these words describe bravura performances. While ballerinas executing triple pirouettes may earn praise for bravura technique, the term still applies mainly to men. Historically, bravura roles were considered "demi-caractère." Performed by compact athletic dancers, the performances typically featured pyrotechnical interludes, or divertissement, in the middle of an act.

Once brilliant performers like Mikhail Baryshnikov and Fernando Bujones became internationally celebrated for their combination of explosive physical power and complete physical control, audiences began to expect speed and dazzle as much as elegant partnering. Bravura no longer was relegated to a supporting role. In fact, Baryshnikov's exuberant staging of *Don Quixote* for ABT put it front and center stage. Barrel turns and soaring leaps became de rigueur in male variations. Today, bravura dancers' crowd-pleasing qualities have given them even greater prominence in the roster of international stars. Artistry, however, remains at the core of the greatest performance. "Bravura has nothing to do with technique," says Kevin McKenzie. "It's all about timing and oozing life."

"I just explode in roles like the slave in *Le Corsaire*. I don't even know what I've done. All I can remember is this blast of energy going through me."

At the heart of classical ballet lies a romantic ideal stretching back to the age of chivalry. The ballerina is the lady, adored and revered, and her partner is her knight, tender and solicitous. From this chivalric tradition springs the term danseur noble. The dancer presents his lady to the audience with grace and courtesy, and gallantly makes her the admired center of all eyes.

"The noble entitlement bespeaks an élan, a certain type of relationship with your partner," says Kevin McKenzie. "It means formidable technique not displayed lightly. The excitement comes from elegance." Projecting that particular constellation of qualities takes more than height and good looks, and noble dancers are the rarest breed. A noble dancer has great clarity and control in executing steps, and great sensitivity as a partner. While dance lovers will endlessly debate whether a certain dancer belongs in one category of dancer or another, most would agree that Erik Bruhn, Ivan Nagy, and Anthony Dowell embody the noble ideal. There are others just as notable, and many more who have noble qualities. And there are dancers like Jose Manuel Carreno (left), who straddle bravura and noble roles gracefully.

"A danseur noble is above all a gentleman when it comes to his partner."

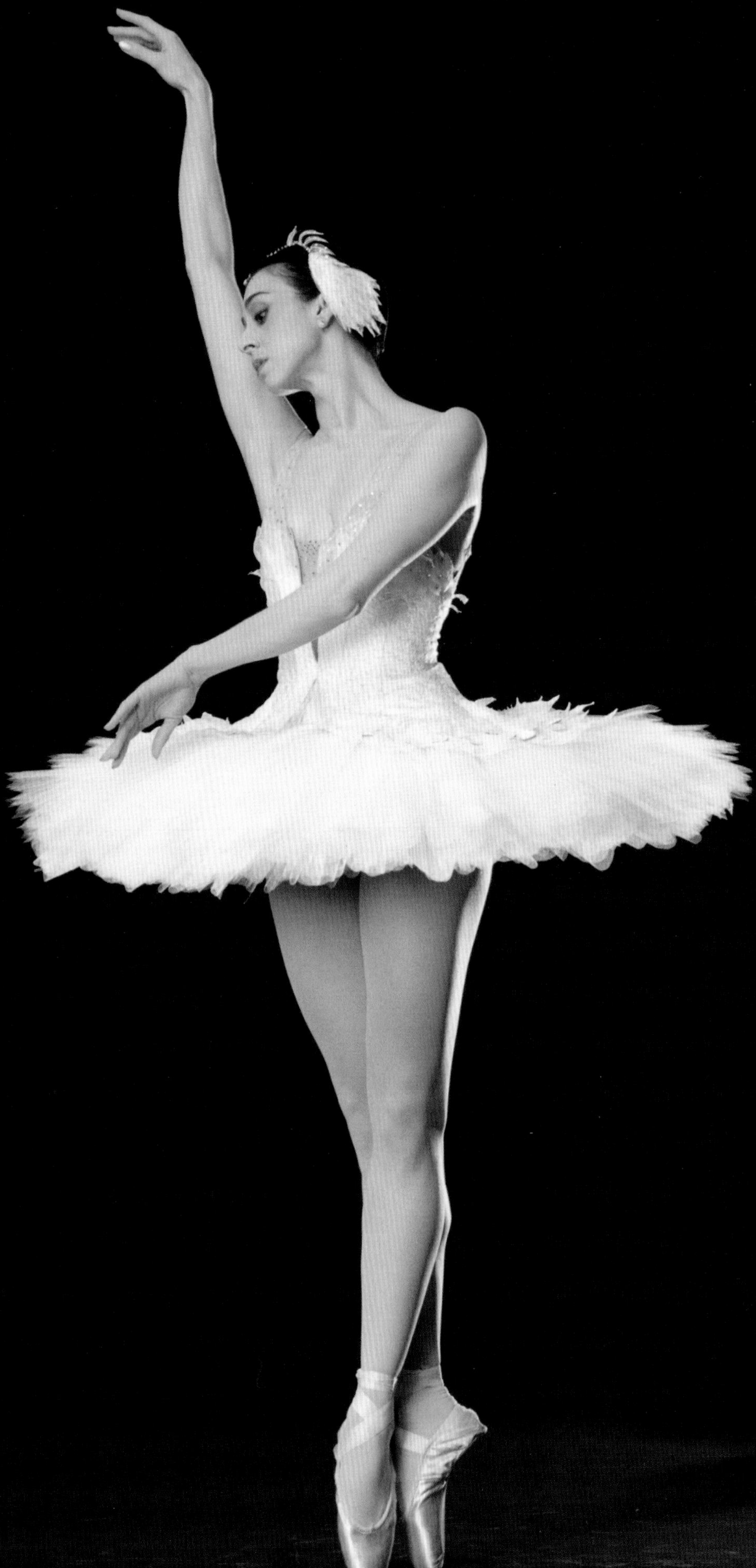

"Lyrical" often alternates with adagio when describing a ballerina gifted in performing the languorous pas de deux and graceful variations that dominate so many classical ballets. "An adagio ballerina must have a level of comfort with sustained, expansive movement," says McKenzie. She must have strength, amplitude, and a striking extension. An adagio ballerina can hold a position with clarity and confidence, keeping her balance a second or two longer than expected. She can project tenderness and yearning in a pas de deux. She has a regal grace and glamour that make the fairytale elements of a ballet seem credible.

Labels do little to convey the qualities of the great lyrical ballerinas. Among those who have excelled in adagio roles are former ABT principal Martine van Hamel, Carla Fracci, Natalia Markarova, and Nina Ananiashvili, shown at left.

"Ballet is not just movement, not simply abstract. It's something beautiful. Sometimes there's this feeling in the moment itself that makes me want to cry."

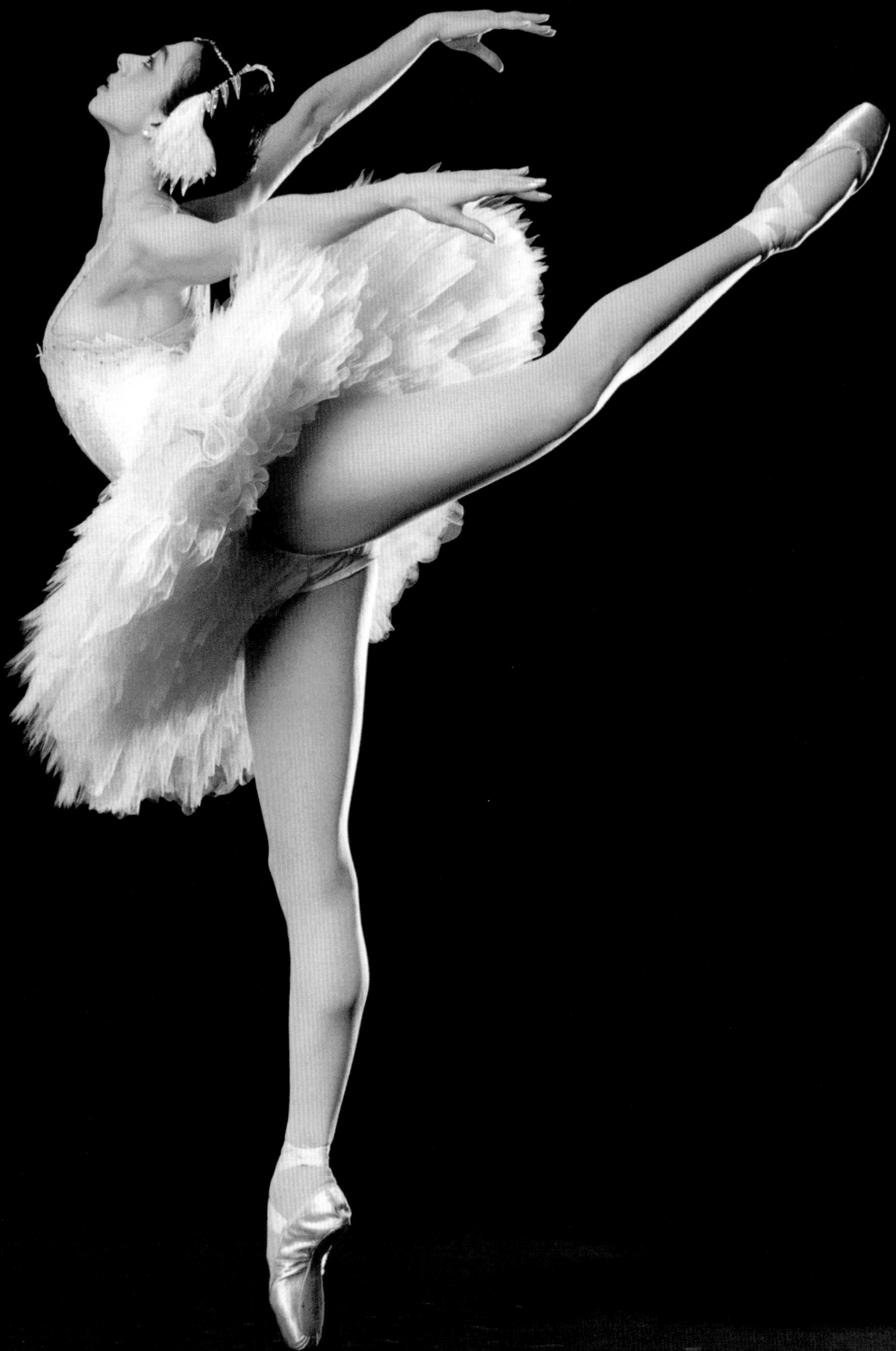

In music, allegro means "quick," as it does in ballet. "An allegro dancer has incredible speed and clarity. It's not second nature to everyone," says McKenzie. An allegro ballerina must turn at superhuman speeds, jump higher than seems possible, and execute steps that are fast and complicated with brio. Allegro roles tend to be the soubrette parts. They require a certain sparkle, both in technique and in presentation. Charm, piquancy, and freshness in an accomplished allegro ballerina can make a performance truly entertaining. Among those who triumphed in allegro roles are Margot Fonteyn and Maya Plisetskaya. Paloma Herrera (left), who has danced a wide range of roles, first achieved acclaim as the flirtatious Kitri in *Don Quixote*, a quintessential allegro role.

"It's not pure classicism versus soubrette charm anymore. It should all be part of your package, but you'll still be known for certain qualities."

There is a rich storytelling tradition in ballet that relies on acting and pantomime. While some of those mime passages may fall to the ballerina or her partner, often they belong to another dancer altogether, who may not even have a prominent place on the program. This "character" dancer may portray a stern father seeking a match for a flighty daughter, or an evil witch determined to bring a young man to ruin. It's a ballet tradition for male dancers to portray caricatures of older women, whether it's the evil witch in *La Sylphide* or the evil fairy in *The Sleeping Beauty*, or the bullying mother in *La Fille Mal Gardée*. The role may be broadly comic, or subtly poignant, but how it is rendered will shade the ballet's performance. "The character roles in ballet are the catalysts," says soloist Ethan Brown, who has won praise for his thoughtful interpretations.

In the Russian ballet tradition, character dancing involves completely separate training and coaching, but at ABT, company members dance these roles based on their dramatic abilities. "We can astound the audience with our technique and the cleverness of the choreography," says Victor Barbee, a celebrated character dancer as well as the company's assistant artistic director, "but there's that other aspect—feeling. You can try to make people feel things they don't every day." Mime requires skill and timing to be understood by the entire audience without seeming broad or inappropriate to the ballet's style. While some gestures, like swearing an oath or shaking a fist, have universal meaning, others may be choreographed for a certain role. "You can't just go through the motions," says Brown. "As I perform a part, I tell myself what I'm trying to show the audience. When I dance Hilarion in *Giselle*, I'm saying to myself, 'This is the girl that I love.' If you believe what you're saying, it'll read out front." Barbee has a similar view. "A simple mime gesture can say something pure and believable, something not expressed as well in pure dance movement."

This mime passage (top row, left) from *La Fille Mal Gardée* reveals the coquettish Lise's secret wish to be married and have children. She sees herself in years to come raising and scolding them. Unlike many mime sequences that allow the dancer to bring their own coloring and interpretation to the passage, these gestures were choreographed by Frederick Ashton to fit into the ballet's comic tone.

These mime gestures (bottom row, left), which represent listening, knocking, questioning, and refusing, appear in various ballets including *Giselle* and *The Sleeping Beauty*.

Oaths of love (top
row, left) often le[ad]
to tragedy in class[ic]
ballet. A mime pas-
sage from *Le Corsa[ire]*
(middle row) show[s]
some universally
familiar bargainin[g]
body language:
Will there be a de[al?]
On the bottom ro[w]
the debate turns
threatening.

The works of one or two choreographers form the foundation of many ballet companies' repertory. Performing these works year in, year out, shapes the dancers' style and gives the company a distinct identity. The Royal Danish Ballet has the nineteenth-century masterpieces of August Bournonville for a touchstone. New York City Ballet has the works of George Balanchine. England's Royal Ballet mounts frequent productions of works by Kenneth MacMillan and Frederick Ashton. Preserving these ballets' creative integrity gives the company an institutional mission as well as a devoted audience.

A WINDOW ON NEW TALENT

ABT's history includes many notable choreographers, but no single shaping choreographic influence. The company's repertory has always mixed classical and contemporary. When Lucia Chase founded ABT in 1940, it reflected the range of her taste, which veered from romantic nineteenth-century classics like *Giselle* to the buoyant Americana of Agnes de Mille. "When the company began, it was like a museum of ballet that kept a big show window for new choreographic talent," says Francis Mason, editor of *Ballet Review* and author with George Balanchine of *101 Stories of the Great Ballets.* "They wanted to live up to their name. Theater is a word that sounds nice, but they meant it. They decided they would be a dance company with dramatic emphasis." The choreographers associated with the company in its first decades—Antony Tudor (*Pillar of Fire*), Agnes de Mille (*Rodeo*), Jerome Robbins (*Fancy Free*)—had an emotional immediacy that few could match. Their works generated tremendous excitement about the young company.

FROM ROMANTIC TO CLASSICAL

With its tale of love and betrayal and its ghostly vampire maidens seeking revenge, *Giselle*, one of the first works to enter ABT's repertory, remains the epitome of a Romantic ballet. Other ballets of the Romantic era, like *La Sylphide*, also play upon the idea of the ballerina as an otherworldly creature, not bound by gravity. Choreography often included leaps and hops on pointe, to remind audiences that the ballerina wasn't earthbound like other mere mortals. The art of ballet was still quite new, and a ballerina who went up on pointe and then performed a series of steps was an instant sensation. Gradually, the choreographic vocabulary evolved a more formal, distilled approach to narrative. The presiding genius of the classical era was a Frenchman, Marius Petipa, who became ballet master in chief to the tsar in 1869. During his many decades in St. Petersburg, Petipa created or staged most of the ballets now at the heart of the classical repertory: *La Bayadère*, *The Sleeping Beauty*, *Swan Lake*, *The Nutcracker*. All deploy dancers—in groups, pairs, or solos—in an architectural sculpting of the stage space. Bodies form patterns that group and regroup in time to the music. The effect is that of a constantly re-forming human kaleidoscope.

While classical ballets tell a story, mime and plot are often secondary to the harmony of the dancing. The ballet's meaning is conveyed subtly, and while imbued with emotion, demands little emoting. The interplay even in mime passages often crystallizes into simple gestures—a hand raised in a pledge of love. The white swan pas de deux in *Swan Lake* offers a beautiful example of love unfolding entirely through a series of elegant lifts and balances. It's one of ballet's most exciting passages, and yet the Prince and Swan Queen rarely face one another. The classical era brought ballet to a new level, one that fused music, choreography, and performance into a single emotional expression.

THE SHOCK OF THE NEW

The Russian Revolution in 1917 officially ended the classical era. Ballet's epicenter shifted to Paris and to impresario Serge Diaghilev. Under his influence in the 1910s and 1920s, ballet emerged as an abstract, symbolic art form, akin to the paintings of Picasso—who occasionally designed sets—and the music of Igor Stravinsky, who sometimes composed scores. It was a radical redefinition, reflected in the choreography of Michel Fokine and George Balanchine, and its influence spread like ripples across the Continent and then the ocean.

In the years that followed, what was once avant-garde became commonplace. Ballets no longer were bound by narrative conventions. Dancers often appeared in leotards and tights. The music and the movement took center stage. Balanchine's influence was immeasurable. It's hard to imagine the impact of a ballet like *Apollo* when it was first performed. Now, it seems almost quaint in its formalism, like a Rockefeller Center bas relief. Many choreographers went in other directions, and many preferred to keep a certain theatricality—and often worked with ABT because the company adhered to a dramatic tradition—but ballet had changed forever.

When ABT opted to perform at the Metropolitan Opera House rather than a smaller theater, the repertory had to accommodate the vastness of the house.

Gradually ABT added Russian classics like *Swan Lake* and *The Sleeping Beauty* to its roster. "The setting tailors the repertory. Something the size of the Met requires ballets that are bigger than life," says Mason. "It's the dimensions of the money as well as the size of stage. You need a larger-scale, old-fashioned repertory to fill it." Today ABT offers signature works from other companies, familiar classics, and new pieces. It's a model that's become popular among other international-caliber companies as the cost of producing new ballets continues to mount.

GISELLE

Libretto by Théophile Gautier;
music by Adolphe Adam;
choreography after Jean Coralli,
Jules Perrot and Marius Petipa;
staged by Kevin McKenzie; dancers:
left, and on pages 205 and 206,
principal dancers Ethan Stiefel and
Amanda McKerrow; next page,
soloist Stella Abrera

This tale of love's redemptive power,
which debuted in 1841, remains the
oldest continually performed ballet.
An innocent peasant girl, Giselle, dies
upon discovering that her aristocratic
lover has betrayed her. When he ven-
tures into the woods to find her grave,
she rises from the dead to save him
from the Wilis, ghostly maidens who
roam the night seeking men to dance
to their death. With its lyrical, deli-
cate choreography and ethereal, otherworldly second act, the ballet represents the Romantic style at its height.

LA BAYADÈRE

Choreographed by Natalia Makarova after
Marius Petipa; music by Ludwig Minkus;
dancers: pages 207–210, principal dancer
Nina Ananiashvili; above and left, soloist
Joaquin De Luz

A temple dancer's forbidden love for
a handsome warrior is set against a lavish
dose of late-nineteenth-century spectacle.
Natalia Makarova's landmark 1980 production restored this rarely performed ballet to
its full three acts, and revealed it as a bridge
between the romantic and classical eras. The
famous "Kingdom of the Shades" in Act II,
where the corps de ballet, all in white tutus,
slowly descend a ramp arabesque by
arabesque, established the purity and movement structure that would lie at the heart of
the classical ballets that Petipa was soon to
create.

213

Libretto by Ivan A. Vsevolozhsky and Marius Petipa; choreography by Marius Petipa; music by Peter Ilyitch Tchaikovsky; staging and additional choreography by Kenneth MacMillan; dancers: below and right, principal dancers Nina Ananiashvili and Julio Bocca; next page, soloists Maria Riccetto and Gennadi Saveliev.

The fairy tale of a lovely princess cruelly enchanted on her sixteenth birthday offers ballerinas one of the most technically demanding roles. In the first act, during the celebrated Rose Adagio, Princess Aurora must turn slowly in an attitude on pointe with one hand in her cavalier's, then release his hand and pose four consecutive times without going off pointe. The ballet has a number of divertissements, including the Blue Bird pas de deux, often a showcase for up-and-coming dancers.

215

Choreography by Kevin McKenzie after Marius Petipa and Lev Ivanov; music by Peter Ilyitch Tchaikovsky; dancers: principal dancers Irina Dvorovenko and Maxim Belotserkovsky

The ballet now synonymous with the art itself has been restaged many times. Petipa was not the original choreographer, and most agree that his assistant, Ivanov, improved upon Petipa's staging. Despite the temptation most choreographers Swan Lake has endured and retained its power. The combination of Tchaikovsky's passionate score, the tender wooing of the Swan Queen and the seductive excitement of the Black Swan has proved indestructible. The dual role of Odette/Odile offers classical ballet's greatest technical and interpretive challenge, and a handful of ballerinas have made it their signature. There are many set pieces: the charming synchronized dance of the cygnets in Act II, for one; Odile's thirty-two fouettés, or rapid turns, in the ballroom scene, for another. But the ballet's strength lies in the fusion of its elements, not in a single performance—a modern paradox at the heart of a nineteenth-century masterpiece.

Choreographed by Kevin McKenzie;
music by Peter Ilyitch Tchaiskovsky;
dancers: principal dancers Gillian
Murphy and Marcelo Gomes

   Nearly every ballet company has its
own version of this E.T.A Hoffman
story, which has become an obligatory
holiday staple. ABT's lavishly-staged
version uses none of the traditional
Petipa choreography. The mysterious,
magical Drosselmeyer, the menacing
Rat King, and the Sugar Plum fairy
dance new steps, though Clara and her
Nutcracker prince still visit a land of
sugarplums and flowers before she
awakens from her dream.

223

Choreography by Marius Petipa and
Alexander Gorsky; staged by Kevin
McKenzie and Susan Jones; music by
Ludwig Minkus; principal dancer Jose
Manuel Carreño plays the role of Basil
The flirtatious Kitri and her beloved
Basil may make only cameo appearances
in the novel, but here their rollicking
romance takes up the entire ballet.
The knight is a world-weary onlooker
who tries to help them outfox Kitri's
stubborn father. All ends happily, after a
flurry of Spanish-style dances and the
most competitive partnering in classical
ballet. Kitri and Basil toss off variation
after variation, each seeking to draw
more applause, only to reunite in a series
of breathtaking fish dives and single-
handed lifts that hold the ballerina high
above her partner's head as she shakes
a tambourine.

227

Choreography by Konstantin Sergeyev, after
Marius Petipa; music by Adolphe Adam, Cesare
Pugni, Leo Delibes, Riccardo Drigo, and Prince
Oldenbourg; libretto by Jules-Henri Vernoy de
Saint-Georges and Joseph Mazilier; staging by
Anna-Marie Holmes after Petipa and Sergeyev;
dancers: above and on pages 233–234, guest
artist Carlos Acosta and principal dancer
Paloma Herrera; left and on pages 229–230,
principal dancer Angel Corella; on pages
231–232, principal dancers Vladimir Malakov
and Xiomara Reyes

This breezy pastiche, based so loosely on
Byron's poem as to be unrecognizable, creates one
brilliant showcase after another for male bravura
dancing. Its pirates, slave drivers and harem girls
can't stop tossing off breathtaking solos, and
after a while, the plot simply ceases to matter.
Rarely performed outside Russia until the end of
the Cold War, the ballet's slave pas de trois in Act
II and jardin animé in Act III—a fantasy "gar-
den" of waltzing ballerinas—are among its justly
celebrated moments.

233

Choreography by Victor Gsovsky; staged by Oleg Briansk; music by Daniel Francois Auber; dancers: corps de ballet member David Hallberg and soloist Michele Wiles

This technically demanding pas de deux is an homage to Marius Petipa and the grand classical tradition. It requires the ballerina to perform very slow controlled fouettés and her partner to achieve all-but-superhuman elevation in his jumps. Though critics often find it flashy, its showcase quality makes it a popular competition piece.

Choreography by George Balanchine;
staged by Karin von Aroldingen
and Richard Tanner; music by Igor
Stravinsky; dancers: Guillaume
Graffin, left; Julio Bocca, right

Many male dancers dream of performing this early Balanchine masterpiece.
Tautly choreographed, the ballet reveals
the young god at the moment that he
realizes the full extent of his power.
There is no traditional plot: Apollo dances
with three Muses and by the end, they
have become his handmaidens. The role
requires complete control and precision
on the part of the man, and speed and
dynamism from the women. Balanchine
staged or created several ballets for ABT
in the company's early years; *Apollo*'s place
in the repertory dates back to 1943.

239

Choreography by George Balanchine;
music by Sergei Prokofiev; staged
by Richard Tanner; libretto by Boris
Kochno; dancers: principal dancers
Angel Corella and Paloma Herrera
This stylized version of the biblical
parable, first staged by Balanchine in
1929, has been another favorite of
male dancers. Balanchine tells the story
largely in symbols and gestures, making
one of his few narrative ballets virtually abstract. The incredible jumps choreographed for the Prodigal, combined
with brilliant dancing in the role of the
predatory Siren, can turn an otherwise
dated piece into a tour-de-force.

241

Choreography by Agrippina
Vaganova; staged by Rudolf Nureyev;
music by Cesare Pugni; pictured
dancer: guest artist Carlos Acosta

This Soviet-era pas de deux has a
glancing connection to the Greek myth
of the virginal moon goddess seduced
by the virile hunter, though the costumes certainly give a nod to the story.
With its expansive jumps and acrobatic
balances, it's a popular showpiecefor
virtuoso dancers. It's a piece that often
appears on mixed bills as the heart-
pumping showstopper in the middle
of a program.

Adapted from "A Midsummer Night's Dream" by William Shakespeare; choreography by Frederick Ashton; staging by Anthony Dowell with Christopher Carr; music by Felix Mendelssohn; pictured dancer: soloist Herman Cornejo

Ashton's version of "Midsummer Night's Dream," rarely performed in the United States, offers a wealth of narrative detail, character dancing, and theatrical charm. Concealed beneath the costumes and humor are bravura interludes for the dancers performing the roles Titania and Oberon, and high-jumping antics from Puck. In one famous scene, Ashton puts the enchanted Bottom on pointe, treating audiences to the unusual spectacle of a male dancer executing a tricky comedic solo on the very tips of his toes, which creates an eerie hoof-like effect.

245

**Choreography by Kenneth MacMillan;
staged by Julie Lincoln; music by Sergei
Prokofiev; pictured dancers: principal
dancers Alessandra Ferri and Julio Bocca**

Shakespeare's young lovers hurl themselves
through this dance-drama. The sweeping
music complements MacMillan's sweeping
choreography, which is punctuated by
thrilling lifts and leaps amid the pageantry.
The balcony scene almost equals the ardor of
Shakespeare's language, and while the ballerina's roles isn't technically difficult, the male
dancer's role requires tremendous strength for
the many lifts.

255

Choreography by John Cranko; staged by Reid Anderson and Jane Bourne; music by Peter Ilyitch Tchaikovsky; pictured dancers: former principal dancer Susan Jaffe and soloist Carlos Molina

Cranko takes Pushkin's unhappy, self-centered hero and makes his passion for Tatiana, a lost love, the dramatic heart of the story. An intensely theatrical ballet, Onegin is a showcase for senior dancers who have honed their artistry and understand the many ways to convey emotion in phrasing and expression. Cranko, a contemporary of Kenneth MacMillan, spent his early professional years at the Royal Ballet and created a handful of strong narrative works that have become opera-house staples.

Choreography and direction by Kenneth MacMillan; staged by Monica Parker, Patricia Ruanne, and Wendy Walker; music by Jules Massenet; pictured dancers: principal dancer Julie Kent and former principal dancer Robert Hill

Darkly sensual, this ballet with its seductive, corruptible heroine and louche milieu, has always been a controversial ballet. It tells the same story as Massenet's opera *Manon*, although it does not use the same music. Its demanding choreography includes several pas de deux that require breathtaking partnering. The roles offer a strong showcase for men and women with real star power and the frequently-excerpted bedroom pas de deux in Act II is a thrilling display of long, sinuous extensions, complicated lifts, and playful allure.

259

Choreography by Anthony Tudor; music by Antonin Dvorak; dancer: principal dancer Amanda McKerrow

Antony Tudor created the spare, psychological dance-dramas, most one act in length, that helped to shape ABT's identity in the company's early years. This ballet, a late piece made shortly before his death, is a purely abstract meditation on a woman at life's turning point, looking back towards youth and ahead toward death. One of the last ballets Tudor choreographed, it has an underlying melancholy.

THE LEAVES ARE FADING

Saying farewell can be harder than making a debut. For principal dancer Susan Jaffe, the finale to her ballet career meant nearly as much as the years of performing that preceded it. Leaving the world of ballet meant venturing into unknown territory, although that had an allure. "It felt like jumping off a cliff a lot of days, but I needed something new," Jaffe remembers.

Dance is life for someone who becomes a star. To leave behind the music, the choreography, and most of all, the audience, can be hard. For Jaffe, whose career began when she was still in her teens, the stage was home and American Ballet Theatre was family. While she knew she might keep ties to the company in one capacity or another, she felt that her new life would be far different.

The realization that the future might include yet unimagined opportunities didn't ease the intensity of the break. Jaffe knew she would teach ballet, a tradition as well as a second career of many of the world's leading ballerinas, including Jaffe's own coach, Kirov Ballet legend Irina Kolpakova. She knew she would continue to show young dancers what she had learned and help them interpret their roles more dramatically, a passion of hers, but all that was still to come.

Jaffe gave her final performance in *Giselle*. As she waited in the wings for her music, she realized when the curtain came down that she would no longer be a ballerina. "Every other performance, there was always a next day. You could always make it better," she recalls. For a few seconds, she felt too weak to dance. Then she heard the notes leading up to Giselle's entrance and decided to savor the moments ahead. As she stepped one more time into the spotlight, the audience burst into overwhelming applause.

Now in the midst of exploring new roles as a teacher and administrator, Jaffe looks back fondly on what always will be a night apart. "Dancers are lucky. Unlike so many people, we get to have two careers," she says. "I look forward to who I'll become next."

A haunting evening of dancing ended in forty-five minutes of ovations, as the audience reluctantly bid a favorite good-bye. After a long company party, Jaffe and a few dancers came down at 2 a.m. to the empty stage. "It was dark, eerie," she remembers. "There was the second-act set, and a single bulb burning on the stage. The whole empty theater was in front of us. I was so grateful at that moment it had been a part of my life."

First, I want to thank my incredible husband, for his patience, good humor, and his fabulous eye for the finer points of ballet. (Who knew?!) Our assistant Angela Titolo, for taking every last-minute request with grace. To my photo assistant Ken Ferdman and my seconds Luke Stoecker and James Matthews: Ken, who is always calm and together, made our sessions seamless and in focus! My printers John Erdman and Gary Schneider, for their impeccable processing and black-and-white print making, Green Rhino for the beautiful color, and to Sixty Eight Degrees for their last-minute help. Special thanks to Paul Kolnik for the use of his photograph.

Thank you to my editors Alex Tart and Holly Rothman, who kept the "Wild Things" on track, Bonnie Eldon and Rebecca Cremenese for their care in preparing the book for production, and Charles Miers, our publisher, who knows ballet and soccer and loves them both!

To Hanna Rubin, for her endless hours of interviews and rewriting as certain section were reformulated. And to Chuck Davidson, our brilliant art director, who has always made my work look better! Only he could have held the complexity of our project in design order.

However, this book would not exist were it not for the incredible dancers, artistic staff, and everyone who lives to make American Ballet Theatre the great international company it is. A big thanks to Kevin McKenzie, Artistic Director, whose insight, good humor, and improvisations gave so much energy to this book—it is not often an Artistic Director, at the whim of a photographer, teaches class. And to Susan Jaffe, who selflessly gave invaluable help to our project.

Thanks also to Victor Barbee, Assistant Artistic Director, who shepherded all the photo sessions. Ballet Masters Guillaume Graffin, Susan Jones, Irina Kolpakova, Georgina Parkinson, and Kirk Peterson, who all brought their skill to our pages. Choreographer Lar Lubovitch, who worked on "Valentine" specifically for this project. Clinton Luckett, for his creative consulting. Wally Chappell, Mary Jo Ziesel, Olga Dvorovenko, John Meehan, our makeup artist Riva Pizhadze, Bruce Horowitz our wardrobe supervisor and his team, Hilarie Jenkins,

Frederick Franklin   Susan Jones   Victor Barbee   Kirk Peterson   Kevin McKenzie   Guillaume Graffin   Georgina Parkinson   Irina Kolpakova

Caryn Conway, and Dennis Ballard, Tina Escoda, Rhoda Oster, Myra Armstrong, Kelly Ryan, Peter Lyden, and Rosalie O'Connor for their help.

Thank you to our enchanting young dancer, Alexandra Dobles. Liz Kehler, Gerry Grinberg, and Lewis Ranieri have given our project incredible support on the Board level. I will be forever grateful.

But, finally, it is to the dancers that I owe my most profound gratitude. It is my love of American Ballet Theatre and total dedication to capturing their beauty, skill, athleticism, and spirituality that inspired the book.

I hope the camera does indeed capture the soul, for each dancer brought their heart and soul to this project. Their artistry gives our book its life force, and I remain in awe of their talent. There were so many exquisite images. Not all could be included. I wish they had.

-Nancy Ellison

In preparing the text for this book, I turned frequently to Robert Greskovic's invaluable *Ballet 101* and George Balanchine and Francis Mason's *101 Stories of the Great Ballets*. I would like to thank Lupe Serrano, Clinton Luckett, and Nina Gross for patiently explaining many ballet training fundamentals, and ABT Director of Press Kelly Ryan and Manager of Press Farah Lopez for their considerable help. Special thanks to Susan Jaffe and to both my editors at Rizzoli, Holly Rothman and Alex Tart, for their excellent fine tuning. Many thanks as well to Nancy Ellison for inviting me to be part of such a beautiful project and Chuck Davidson for making a wonderful frame for it all.

This text is for my parents, Enid and Isaiah Rubin, and for George and Ruth Gross, who first showed me the beauty that is ballet.

-Hanna Rubin

Lewis Ranieri   Gedalio Grinberg   Tina Escoda   Florence Pettan   Rhoda Oster